The Wisdom of
MARK TWAIN

Also available from The Wisdom Library

THE WISDOM OF JOHN ADAMS
THE WISDOM OF BUDDHA
THE WISDOM OF CONFUCIUS
THE WISDOM OF GEORGE ELIOT
THE WISDOM OF SIGMUND FREUD
THE WISDOM OF GANDHI
THE WISDOM OF GIBRAN
THE WISDOM OF CARL JUNG
THE WISDOM OF THE KABBALAH
THE WISDOM OF OMAR KHAYYAM
THE WISDOM OF THE KORAN
THE WISDOM OF MAO
THE WISDOM OF KARL MARX
THE WISDOM OF MUHAMMAD
THE WISDOM OF THEODORE ROOSEVELT
THE WISDOM OF BERTRAND RUSSELL
THE WISDOM OF THE SAINTS
THE WISDOM OF SARTRE
THE WISDOM OF SHAKESPEARE
THE WISDOM OF THE TALMUD
THE WISDOM OF THOREAU
THE WISDOM OF LEO TOLSTOY
THE WISDOM OF THE TORAH
THE WISDOM OF OSCAR WILDE

Published by Citadel Press

The Wisdom of
MARK TWAIN

EDITED BY SEYMOUR BAROFSKY

PHILOSOPHICAL LIBRARY

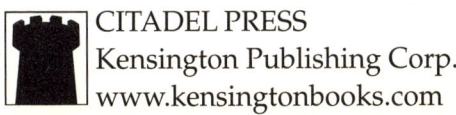

CITADEL PRESS
Kensington Publishing Corp.
www.kensingtonbooks.com

CITADEL PRESS BOOKS are published by

Kensington Publishing Corp.
850 Third Avenue
New York, NY 10022

Copyright © 2003 The Philosophical Library, Inc.
Selection copyright © 2003 Seymour Barofsky

All rights reserved. No part of this book may be reproduced in any form or by any means without the prior written consent of the publisher, excepting brief quotes used in reviews.

Titles included in the Wisdom Library are published by arrangement with Philosophical Library.

All Kensington titles, imprints, and distributed lines are available at special quantity discounts for bulk purchases for sales promotions, premiums, fund raising, educational, or institutional use. Special book excerpts or customized printings can also be created to fit specific needs. For details, write or phone the office of the Kensington special sales manager: Kensington Publishing Corp., 850 Third Avenue, New York, NY 10022, attn: Special Sales Department, phone 1-800-221-2647.

CITADEL PRESS and the Citadel logo are Reg. U.S. Pat. & TM Off.

First Wisdom Library printing: August 2003

10   9   8   7   6   5   4   3   2   1

Printed in the United States of America

Library of Congress Control Number: 2003100616

ISBN 0-8065-2505-3

CONTENTS

Editor's Preface   xi

I. Introduction

    "I am not here to deceive; I am here to teach"   3
    (From an address delivered on Twain's seventieth birthday, December 5, 1905)

II. Boys and Girls

    "You do a girl tolerable poor"   13
    (From *Adventures of Huckleberry Finn*, Chapter 11)

    Advice to Youth   21
    (Address delivered on April 15, 1882)

    The Story of the Bad Little Boy   25
    (In *Sketches New and Old*)

    The Story of the Good Little Boy   29
    (In *Sketches New and Old*)

GIRLS 35
(Address delivered on February 10, 1887)

THE BABIES 37
(Address delivered on November 13, 1879)

III. The Human Condition

CONCLUSION 43
(From *What Is Man? And Other Essays*)

THE LADIES 50
(An address delivered in November 1873)

THE FIVE BOONS OF LIFE 54
(In *The $30,000 Bequest*)

THE TURNING POINT OF MY LIFE 57
(*Harpers Bazar*, February 1910)

IV. America and Americans

PLYMOUTH ROCK AND THE PILGRIMS 71
(From an address delivered on
December 22, 1881)

THE WEATHER 77
(Address delivered on December 22, 1876)

NEW YORK CITY 81
(From an address delivered on
December 6, 1906)

TAXES AND MORALS 84
(From an address delivered on
January 22, 1906)

CHARACTERISTICS OF AMERICANS 86
(From "What Mr. Paul Bourget Thinks of Us,"
North American Review, January 1895)

DISGRACEFUL PERSECUTION OF A BOY 99
(In *Galaxy,* May 1870)

THE PRIVATE HISTORY OF A CAMPAIGN
THAT FAILED 104
(In *The American Claimant*)

V. Religion and the Moral Order

ABOUT SMELLS 129
(In *Galaxy,* May 1870)

REFLECTIONS ON THE SABBATH 132
(In *San Francisco Golden Era,* March 18, 1866)

HOW I BECAME INTERESTED IN SATAN 135
(From *Is Shakespeare Dead?*)

THEORETICAL AND PRACTICAL MORALS 138
(Address delivered on July 8, 1899)

JOURNEY TO DAMASCUS 142
(From Chapter 43, *Innocents Abroad*)

AS CONCERNS INTERPRETING THE DEITY 145
(In *What Is Man? And Other Essays*)

BENARES 155
(*Following the Equator,* Chapter 51)

Contents

VI. The Social Order

    THE BEE   167
    (In *What Is Man? And Other Essays*)

    A CURIOUS SCRAP OF HISTORY   172
    (In *Harper's Magazine,* October 1914)

VII. Literature and Art

    HOW TO TELL A STORY   183
    (In *The $30,000 Bequest*)

    DISAPPEARANCE OF LITERATURE   190
    (Address delivered November 20, 1900)

    THE LICENSE OF ART   193
    (*A Tramp Abroad,* Chapter 50)

VIII. The World at Large

    IMPERIAL HONORS TO AN AMERICAN   201
    (From *The Innocents Abroad,* Chapter 15)

    SNOBS, AT HOME AND ABROAD   203
    (From *The Innocents Abroad,* Chapter 23)

    MICHELANGELO   206
    (From *The Innocents Abroad,* Chapter 27)

    SOCIABLE ARMENIAN GIRLS   209
    (From *The Innocents Abroad,* Chapter 38)

Contents

THE MAJESTIC SPHINX 212
(From *The Innocents Abroad*, Chapter 58)

ARRIVAL OF MISSIONARIES 216
(*Roughing It*, Chapter 72)

JUDICIOUS MR. RHODES 222
(From *Following the Equator*, Chapter 68)

EDITOR'S PREFACE

Mark Twain (pseudonym of Samuel Langhorne Clemens) was born in Florida, Missouri, on November 30, 1835, and died on April 10, 1910, in Connecticut, where he had made his home from 1871. After leaving Hannibal, the Missouri town in which he had spent his childhood, Twain worked on a Mississippi steamboat and for much of the rest of his life traveled extensively, through America and around the world, commenting on the places and the people he encountered. He was a journalist, a travel writer, a philosopher, a humorist, an accomplished public speaker and, above all, a storyteller and novelist.

In selecting pieces from an enormous body of work—written and spoken—that might fall under the rubric of wisdom, it was necessary for a volume of this scope to omit much more than it includes. Insofar as possible, the volume tries to include pieces complete in themselves, or nearly so. With the exception of one excerpt, Twain's novels—even his greatest, *Adventures of Huckleberry Finn*—are not represented here. In any case, they are perhaps best read whole. What this book seeks to present is a sampling of Twain's wisdom—explicit and implicit, funny and entertaining, troubling and thought provoking—about the world he lived in, its people and its ideas—a world still recognizable in ours.

I.

INTRODUCTION

"I AM NOT HERE TO DECEIVE; I AM HERE TO TEACH"*

I have had a great many birthdays in my time. I remember the first one very well, and I always think of it with indignation; everything was so crude, unaesthetic, primeval. Nothing like this at all. No proper appreciative preparation made; nothing really ready. Now, for a person born with high and delicate instincts—why, even the cradle wasn't whitewashed—nothing ready at all. I hadn't any hair, I hadn't any teeth, I hadn't any clothers, I had to go to my first banquet just like that. Well, everybody came swarming in. It was the merest little bit of a village—hardly that, just a little hamlet, in the backwoods of Missouri, where nothing ever happened, and the people were all interested, and they all came; they looked me over to see if there was anything fresh in my line. Why, nothing ever happened in that village—I—why, I was the only thing that had really happened there for months and months and months; and although I say it myself that shouldn't, I came the nearest to being a real event that had happened in that village in more than two years. Well, those people came, they came with that curiosity which is so provincial, with that frankness which is also so provincial, and they examined me all around and gave their opinion. Nobody asked them, and I shouldn't have minded if anybody had paid me a compliment, but nobody did. Their opinions were all just green with preju-

*Editor's title.

dice, and I feel those opinions to this day. Well I stood that as long as—well, you know I was born courteous, and I stood it to the limit. It stood it an hour, and then the worm turned. I was the worm; it was my turn to turn, and I turned. I knew very well the strength of my position; I knew that I was the only spotlessly pure and innocent person in that whole town, and I came out and said so. And they could not say a word. It was so true. They blushed; they were embarrassed. Well, that was the first after-dinner speech I ever made. I think it was after dinner.

It's a long stretch between that first birthday speech and this one. That was my cradle-song, and this is my swan-song, I suppose. I am used to swan-songs; I have sung them several times.

This is my seventieth birthday, and I wonder if you all rise to the size of that proposition, realizing all the significance of that phrase, seventieth birthday.

The seventieth birthday! It is the time of life when you arrive at a new and awful dignity; when you may throw aside the decent reserves which have oppressed you for a generation and stand unafraid and unabashed upon your seven-terraced summit and look down and teach—unrebuked. You can tell the world how you got there. It is what they all do. You shall never get tired of telling by what delicate arts and deep moralities you climbed up to that great place. You will explain the process and dwell on the particulars with senile rapture. I have been anxious to explain my own system this long time, and now at last I have the right.

I have achieved my seventy years in the usual way: by sticking strictly to a scheme of life which would kill anybody else. It sounds like an exaggeration, but that is really the common rule for attaining to old age. When we examine the programme of any of these garrulous old people we always find that the habits which have preserved them would have decayed us; that the way of life which enabled them to live upon the property of their heirs so long, as Mr. Choate says, would have put us out of commission ahead of time. I will offer here, as a sound maxim, this: That we can't reach old age by another man's road.

I will now teach, offering my way of life to whomsoever desires to commit suicide by the scheme which has enabled me to beat the doctor and the hangman for seventy years. Some of the details may sound untrue, but they are not. I am not here to deceive; I am here to teach.

We have no permanent habits until we are forty. Then they begin to harden, presently they petrify, then business begins. Since forty I have been regular about going to bed and getting up—and that is one of the main things. I have made it a rule to go to bed when there wasn't anybody left to sit up with; and I have made it a rule to get up when I had to. This has resulted in an unswerving regularity of irregularity. It has saved me sound, but it would injure another person.

In the matter of diet—which is another main thing—I have been persistently strict in sticking to the things which didn't agree with me until one or the other of us got the best of it. Until lately I got the best of it myself. But last spring I stopped frolicking with mince-pie after midnight: up to then I had always believed it wasn't loaded. For thirty years I have taken coffee and bread at eight in the morning, no bite nor sup until seven-thirty in the evening. Eleven hours. That is all right for me, and is wholesome, because I never had a headache in my life, but headachy people would not reach seventy comfortably by that road, and they would be foolish to try it. And I wish to urge upon you this—which I think is wisdom—that if you find you can't make seventy by any but an uncomfortable road, don't you go. When they take off the Pullman and retire you to the rancid smoker, put on your things, count your checks, and get out at the first way station where there's a cemetery.

I have made it a rule never to smoke more than one cigar at a time. I have no other restriction as regards smoking. I do not know just when I began to smoke, I only know that it was in my father's lifetime, and that I was discreet. He passed from this life early in 1847, when I was a shade past eleven; ever since then I have smoked publicly. As an example to others, and not that I care for moderation myself, it has always been my rule never to smoke when asleep, and never refrain when awake. It is a good rule. I mean, for me; but some of you know quite well that it wouldn't answer for everybody that's trying to get to be seventy.

I smoke in bed until I have to go to sleep; I wake up in the night, sometimes once, sometimes twice, sometimes three times, and I never waste any of these opportunities to smoke. This habit is so old and dear and precious to me that I would feel as you, sir, would feel if you should lose the only moral you've got—meaning the chairman—if you've got one: I am making no charges. I will grant, here, that I have stopped smoking now and then, for a few months at a time, but it was not on principle, it was only to show off; it was to pulverize those critics who said I was a slave to my habits and could not break my bonds.

To-day it is all of sixty years since I began to smoke the limit. I have never bought cigars with life-belts around them. I early found those were too expensive for me. I have always bought cheap cigars—reasonably cheap, at any rate. Sixty years ago they cost me four dollars a barrel, but my taste has improved, latterly, and I pay seven now. Six or seven. Seven, I think. Yes, it's seven. But that includes the barrel. I often have smoking-parties at my house; but the people who come have always just taken the pledge. I wonder why that is?

As for drinking, I have no rule about that. When the others drink I like to help; otherwise I remain dry, by habit and preference. This dryness does not hurt me, but it could easily hurt you, because you are different. You let it alone.

Since I was seven years old I have seldom taken a dose of medicine, and have still seldomer needed one. But up to seven I lived exclusively on allopathic medicines. Not that I needed them, for I don't think I did; it was for economy; my father took a drug-store for a debt, and it made cod-liver oil cheaper than the other breakfast foods. We had nine barrels of it, and it lasted me seven years. Then I was weaned. The rest of the family had to get along with rhubarb and ipecac and such things, because I was the pet. I was the first Standard Oil Trust. I had it all. By the time the drug-store was exhausted my health was established, and there has never been much the matter with me since. But you know very well it would be foolish for the average child to start for seventy on that basis. It happened to be just the thing for me, but that was merely an accident; it couldn't happen again in a century.

I have never taken any exercise, except sleeping and resting, and I never intend to take any. Exercise is loathsome. And it cannot be any benefit when you are tired; and I am always tired. But let another person try my way, and see where he will come out.

I desire now to repeat and emphasize that maxim: We can't reach old age by another man's road. My habits protect my life, but they would assassinate you.

I have lived a severely moral life. But it would be a mistake for other people to try that, or for me to recommend it. Very few would succeed: you have to have a perfectly colossal stock of morals; and you can't get them on a margin; you have to have the whole thing, and put them in your box. Morals are like an acquirement—like music, like a foreign language, like piety, poker, paralysis—no man is born with them. I wasn't myself, I started poor. I hadn't a single moral. There is hardly a man in this house that is poorer than I was then. Yes, I started like that—the world before me, not a moral in the slot. Not even an insurance moral. I can remember the first one I ever got. I can remember the landscape, the weather, the—I can remember how everything looked. It was an old moral, an old second-hand moral, all out of repair, and didn't fit, anyway. But if you are careful with a thing like that, and keep it in a dry place, and save it for processions, and Chautauquas, and World's Fairs, and so on, and disinfect it now and then, and give it a fresh coat of whitewash once in a while, you will be surprised how well she will last and how long she will keep sweet, or at least inoffensive. When I got that mouldy old moral, she had stopped growing, because she hadn't any exercise; but I worked her hard, I worked her Sundays and all. Under this cultivation, she waxed in might and stature beyond belief, and served me well and was my pride and joy for sixty-three years; then she got to associating with insurance presidents, and lost flesh and character, and was a sorrow to look at and no longer competent for business. She was a great loss to me. Yet not all loss. I sold her—ah, pathetic skeleton, as she was—I sold her to Leopold, the pirate King of Belgium; he sold her to our Metropolitan Museum, and it was very glad to get her, for without a rag on, she stands 57 feet long and 16 feet high, and they think she's a brontosaur. Well, she looks it. They believe it will take nineteen geological periods to breed her match.

Morals are of inestimable value, for every man is born crammed with sin microbes, and the only thing that can extirpate these sin microbes is morals. Now you take a sterilized Christian—I mean, you take *the* sterilized Christian, for there's only one. Dear sir, I wish you wouldn't look at me like that.

Threescore years and ten!

It is the Scriptural statute of limitations. After that, you owe no active duties; for you, the strenuous life is over. You are a time-expired man, to use Kipling's military phrase: You have served your term, well or less well, and you are mustered out. You are become an honorary member of the republic, you are emancipated, compulsions are not for you, nor any bugle-call but "lights out." You pay the time-worn duty bills if you choose, or decline if you prefer—and without prejudice—for they are not legally collectable.

The previous-engagement plea, which in forty years has cost you so many twinges, you can lay aside forever; on this side of the grave you will never need it again. If you shrink at thought of night, and winter, and the late home-coming from the banquet and the lights and the laughter through the deserted streets—a desolation which would not remind you now, as for a generation it did, that your friends are sleeping, and you must creep in a-tiptoe and not disturb them, but would only remind you that you need not tiptoe, you can never disturb them more—if you shrink at the thought of these things, you need only reply, "Your invitation honors me, and pleases me because you still keep me in your remembrance, but I am seventy; seventy, and would nestle in the chimney-corner, and smoke my pipe, and read my book, and take my rest, wishing you well in all affection, and that when you in your return shall arrive at pier No. 70 you may step aboard your waiting ship with a reconciled spirit, and lay your cause toward the sinking sun with a contented heart.

II.

BOYS AND GIRLS

"You do a girl tolerable poor"*

"Come in," says the woman, and I did. She says:
"Take a cheer."
I done it. She looked me all over with her little shiny eyes, and says:
"What might your name be?"
"Sarah Williams."
"Where 'bouts you live? In this neighborhood?"
"No'm. In Hookerville, seven mile below. I've walked all the way and I'm all tired out."
"Hungry, too, I reckon. I'll find you something."
"No'm, I ain't hungry. I was so hungry I had to stop two mile below here at a farm; so I ain't hungry no more. It's what makes me so late. My mother's down sick, and out of money and everything, and I come to tell my uncle Abner Moore. He lives at the upper end of the town, she says. I hain't never been here before. Do you know him?"
"No; but I don't know everybody yet. I haven't lived here quite two weeks. It's a considerable ways to the upper end of the town. You better stay here all night. Take off your bonnet."
"No," I says, "I'll rest a while, I reckon, and go on. I ain't afeard of the dark."
She said she wouldn't let me go by myself; but her husband would be in by-and-by, maybe in a hour and a half,

*Editor's title.

and she'd send him along with me. Then she got to talking about her husband, and about her relations up the river, and her relations down the river, and about how much better off they used to was, and how they didn't know but they'd made a mistake coming to our town, instead of letting well alone—and so on and so on, till I was afeard *I* had made the mistake coming to her to find out what was going on in the town; but by-and-by she dropped onto pap and the murder, and then I was pretty willing to let her clatter right along. She told about me and Tom Sawyer finding the six thousand dollars (only she got it ten) and all about pap and what a hard lot he was, and what a hard lot I was, and at last she got down to where I was murdered. I says:

"Who done it? We've heard considerable about these goings on, down in Hookerville, but we don't know who 'twas that killed Huck Finn."

"Well, I reckon there's a right smart chance of people *here* that'd like to know who killed him. Some thinks old Finn done it himself."

"No—is that so?"

"Most everybody thought it at first. He'll never know how nigh he come to getting lynched. But before the night they changed around and judged it was done by a runaway nigger named Jim."

"Why *he*——"

I stopped. I reckoned I better keep still. She run on, and never noticed I had put in at all.

"The nigger run off the very night Huck Finn was killed. So there's a reward out for him—three hundred dollars. And there's a reward out for old Finn too—two hundred dollars. You see, he come to town the morning after the murder, and told about it, and was out with 'em on the ferry-boat hunt, and right away after he up and left. Before night they wanted to lynch him, but he was gone, you see.

Well, next day they found out the nigger was gone; they found out he hadn't been seen sence ten o'clock the night the murder was done. So then they put it on him, you see, and while they was full of it, next day back comes old Finn and went boo-hooing to Judge Thatcher to get money to hunt for the nigger all over Illinois with. The judge give him some, and that evening he got drunk and was around till after midnight with a couple of mighty hard looking strangers, and then went off with them. Well, he hain't come back sence, and they ain't looking for him back till this thing blows over a little, for people thinks now that he killed his boy and fixed things so folks would think robbers done it, and then he'd get Huck's money without having to bother a long time with a lawsuit. People do say he warn't any too good to do it. Oh, he's sly, I reckon. If he don't come back for a year, he'll be all right. You can't prove anything on him, you know; everything will be quieted down then, and he'll walk into Huck's money as easy as nothing."

"Yes, I reckon so, 'm. I don't see nothing in the way of it. Has everybody quit thinking the nigger done it?"

"Oh, no, not everybody. A good many thinks he done it. But they'll get the nigger pretty soon, now, and maybe they can scare it out of him."

"Why, are they after him yet?"

"Well, you're innocent, ain't you! Does three hundred dollars lay round every day for people to pick up? Some folks thinks the nigger ain't far from here. I'm one of them—but I hain't talked it around. A few days ago I was talking with an old couple that lives next door in the log shanty, and they happened to say hardly anybody ever goes to that island over yonder they call Jackson's Island. Don't anybody live there? says I. No, nobody, says they. I didn't say any more, but I done some thinking. I was pretty near certain I'd seen smoke over there, about the head of the island, a day or two before that, so I says to myself, like as not that nigger's hiding over there; anyways, says I, it's worth the trouble to give the place a hunt. I hain't seen any smoke sence, so I reckon maybe he's gone, if it was him; but my husband's gone over to see—him and another man. He was gone up the river, but he got back to-day and I told him as soon as he got here two hours ago."

I had got so uneasy I couldn't set still. I had to do something with my hands; so I took up a needle off the table and went to threading it. My hands shook, and I was making a bad job of it. When the woman stopped talking, I looked up, and she was looking at me pretty curious, and smiling a little. I put down the needle and thread and let on to be interested—and I was, too—and says:

"Three hundred dollars is a power of money. I wish my mother could get it. Is your husband going over there to-night?"

"Oh, yes. He went up town with the man I was telling you of, to get a boat and see if they could borrow another gun. They'll go over after midnight."

"Couldn't they see better if they was to wait till day-time?"

"Yes. And couldn't the nigger see better, too? After midnight he'll likely be asleep, and they can slip around through the woods and hunt up his campfire all the better for the dark, if he's got one."

"I didn't think of that."

The woman kept looking at me pretty curious, and I didn't feel a bit comfortable. Pretty soon she says:

"What did you say your name was, honey?"

"M—Mary Williams."

Somehow it didn't seem to me that I said it was Mary before, so I didn't look up; seemed to me I said it was Sarah; so I felt sort of cornered, and was afeared maybe I was look-

ing it, too. I wished the woman would say something more; the longer she set still, the uneasier I was. But now she says:
"Honey, I thought you said it was Sarah when you first come in?"
"Oh, yes'm, I did. Sarah Mary Williams. Sarah's my first name. Some calls me Sarah, some calls me Mary."
"Oh, that's the way of it?"
"Yes'm."
I was feeling better, then, but I wished I was out of there, anyway. I couldn't look up yet.

Well, the woman fell to talking about how hard times was, and how poor they had to live, and how the rats was as free as if they owned the place, and so forth, and so on, and then I got easy again. She was right about the rats. You'd see one stick his nose out of a hole in the corner every little while. She said she had to have things handy to throw at them when she was alone, or they wouldn't give her no peace. She showed me a bar of lead, twisted up into a knot, and said she was a good shot with it generly, but she'd wrenched her arm a day or two ago, and didn't know whether she could throw true, now. But she watched for a chance, and directly she banged away at a rat, but she missed him wide, and said "Ouch!" it hurt her arm so. Then she told me to try for the next one. I wanted to be getting away before the old man got back, but of course I didn't let on. I got the thing, and the first rat that showed his nose I let drive, and if he'd a stayed where he was he'd a been a tolerable sick rat. She said that that was first-rate, and she reckoned I would hive the next one. She went and got the lump of lead and fetched it back and brought along a hank of yarn, which she wanted me to help her with. I held up my two hands and she put the hank over them, and went on talking about her and her husband's matters. But she broke off to say:

"Keep your eye on the rats. You better have the lead in your lap, handy."

So she dropped the lump into my lap, just at that moment, and I clapped my legs together on it and she went on talking. But only about a minute. Then she took off the hank and looked me straight in the face, but very pleasant, and says:

"Come, now—what's your real name?"

"Wh-what, mum?"

"What's your real name? Is it Bill, or Tom, or Bob?—or what is it?"

I reckon I shook like a leaf, and I didn't know hardly what to do. But I says:

"Please to don't poke fun at a poor girl like me, mum. If I'm in the way, here, I'll——"

"No, you won't. Set down and stay where you are. I ain't going to hurt you, and I ain't going to tell on you, nuther. You just tell me your secret, and trust me. I'll keep it; and what's more, I'll help you. So'll my old man, if you want him to. You see, you're a runaway 'prentice—that's all. It ain't anything. There ain't any harm in it. You've been treated bad, and you made up your mind to cut. Bless you, child, I wouldn't tell on you. Tell me all about it, now—that's a good boy."

So I said it wouldn't be no use to try to play it any longer, and I would just make a clean breast and tell her everything, but she musn't go back on her promise. Then I told her my father and mother was dead, and the law had bound me to a mean old farmer in the country thirty mile back from the river, and he treated me so bad I couldn't stand it no longer; he went away to be gone a couple of days, and so I took my chance and stole some of his daughter's old clothes, and cleared out, and I had been three nights coming the thirty miles; I traveled nights, and hid day-times and slept, and the bag of bread and meat I carried from home lasted me all the way and I had a plenty. I said I believed my uncle Abner Moore would take care of me, and so that was why I struck out for this town of Goshen.

"Goshen, child? This ain't Goshen. This is St. Petersburg. Goshen's ten mile further up the river. Who told you this was Goshen?"

"Why, a man I met at day-break this morning, just as I was going to turn into the woods for my regular sleep. He told me when the roads forked I must take the right hand, and five mile would fetch me to Goshen."

"He was drunk I reckon. He told you just exactly wrong."

"Well, he did act like he was drunk, but it ain't no matter now. I got to be moving along. I'll fetch Goshen before daylight."

"Hold on a minute. I'll put you up a snack to eat. You might want it."

So she put me up a snack, and says:

"Say—when a cow's laying down, which end of her gets up first? Answer up, prompt, now—don't stop to study over it. Which end gets up first?"

"The hind end, mum."

"Well, then, a horse?"

"The for'rard end, mum."

"Which side of a tree does the most moss grow on?"

"North side."

"If fifteen cows is browsing on a hillside, how many of them eats with their heads pointed in the same direction?"

"The whole fifteen, mum."

"Well, I reckon you *have* lived in the country. I thought maybe you was trying to hocus me again. What's your real name, now?"

"George Peters, mum."

"Well, try to remember it, George. Don't forget and tell me it's Elexander before you go, and then get out by saying it's George-Elexander when I catch you. And don't go about women in that old calico. You do a girl tolerable poor, but you might fool men, maybe. Bless you, child, when you set out to thread a needle, don't hold the thread still and fetch the needle up to it; hold the needle still and poke the thread at it—that's the way a woman most always does; but a man always does 'tother way. And when you throw at a rat or anything, hitch yourself up a tip-toe, and fetch your hand up over your head as awkard as you can and miss your rat about six or seven foot. Throw stiff-armed from the shoulder, like there was a pivot there for it to turn on—like a girl; not from the wrist and elbow with your arm out to one side, like a boy. And mind you, when a girl tries to catch anything in her lap, she throws her knees apart; she don't clap them together, the way you did when you catched the lump of lead. Why, I spotted you for a boy when you was threading the needle; and I contrived the other things just to make certain. Now trot along to your uncle, Sarah Mary Williams George Elexander Peters, and if you get into trouble you send word to Mrs. Judith Loftus, which is me, and I'll do what I can to get you out of it. Keep the river road, all the way, and next time you tramp, take shoes and socks with you. The river road's a rocky one, and your feet'll be in a condition when you get to Goshen, I reckon."

Advice to Youth

Being told I would be expected to talk here, I inquired what sort of a talk I ought to make. They said it should be something suitable to youth—something didactic, instructive, or something in the nature of good advice. Very well. I have a few things in my mind which I have often longed to say for the instruction of the young; for it is in one's tender early years that such things will best take root and be most enduring and most valuable. First, then, I will say to you, my young friends—and I say it beseechingly, urgingly—

Always obey your parents, when they are present. This is the best policy in the long run, because if you don't they will make you. Most parents think they know better than you do, and you can generally make more by humoring that superstition than you can by acting on your own better judgment.

Be respectful to your superiors, if you have any, also to strangers, and sometimes to others. If a person offend you, and you are in doubt whether it was intentional or not, do not resort to extreme measures; simply watch your chance and hit him with a brick. That will be sufficient. If you shall find he had not intended any offense, come out frankly and confess yourself in the wrong when you struck him; acknowledge it like a man and say you didn't mean to. Yes, always avoid violence; in this age of charity and kindliness, the time has gone by for such things. Leave dynamite to the low and unrefined.

Go to bed early, get up early—this is wise. Some authorities say get up with the sun; some others say get up with one thing, some with another. But a lark is really the best thing to get up with. It gives you a splendid reputation with everybody to know that you get up with the lark; and if you get the right kind of lark, and work at him right, you can easily train him to get up at half past nine, every time—it is no trick at all.

Now as to the matter of lying. You want to be very careful about lying; otherwise you are nearly sure to get caught. Once caught, you can never again be, in the eyes of the good and the pure, what you were before. Many a young person has injured himself permanently through a single clumsy and ill-finished lie, the result of carelessness born of incomplete training. Some authorities hold that the young ought not to lie at all. That, of course, is putting it rather stronger than necessary; still, while I cannot go quite as far as that, I do maintain, and I believe I am right, that the young ought to be temperate in the use of this great art until practice and experience shall give them that confidence, elegance, and precision which alone can make the accomplishment graceful and profitable. Patience, diligence, painstaking attention to detail—these are the requirements; these, in time, will make the student perfect; upon these, and upon these only, may he rely as the sure foundation for future eminence. Think what tedious years of study, thought, practice, experience, went to the equipment of that peerless old mater who was able to impose upon the whole world the lofty and sounding maxim that "truth is mighty and will prevail"—the most majestic compound fracture of fact which any of woman born has yet achieved. For the history of our race, and each individual's experience, are sown thick with evidence that a truth is not hard to kill and that a lie told well is immortal. There in Boston is a monument of the man who discovered anesthesia; many people are aware, in these latter days, that that man didn't discover it at all, but stole the discovery from another man. Is this truth mighty, and will it prevail? Ah no, my hearers, the monument is made of hardy material, but the lie it tells will outlast it a million years. An awkward, feeble, leaky lie is a thing which you ought to make it your unceasing study to avoid; such a lie as that has no more real permanence than an average truth. Why, you might as well tell the truth at once and be done with it. A feeble, stupid, preposterous lie will not live two years—except it be a slander upon somebody. It is indestructible, then, of course, but that is no merit of yours. A final word: begin your practice of this gracious and beautiful art early—begin now. If I had begun earlier, I could have learned how.

Never handle firearms carelessly. The sorrow and suffering that have been caused through the innocent but heedless handling of firearms by the young! Only four days ago, right in the next farmhouse to the one where I am spending the summer, a grandmother, old and gray and sweet, one of the loveliest spirits in the land, was sitting at her work, when her young grandson crept in and got down an old, battered, rusty gun which had not been touched for many years and was supposed not to be loaded, and pointed it at her, laughing and threatening to shoot. In her fright she ran screaming and pleading toward the door on the other side of the room; but as she passed him he placed the gun almost against her very breast and pulled the trigger! He had supposed it was not loaded. And he was right—it wasn't. So there wasn't any harm done. It is the only case of that kind I have ever heard of. Therefore, just the same, don't you meddle with old unloaded firearms; they are the most deadly and unerring things that have ever been created by man. You don't have to take any pains at all with them; you don't have to have a rest, you don't have to have even any sights on the gun, you don't have to take aim, even. No, you just pick out a relative and bang away, and you are sure to get him. A youth who can't hit a cathedral at thirty yards with a Gatling gun in three-quarters of an hour, can take up an old empty musket and bag his grandmother every time, at a hundred. Think what Waterloo would have been if one of the armies had been boys armed with old muskets supposed not to be loaded, and the other army had been composed of their female relations. The very thought of it makes one shudder.

There are many sorts of books; but good ones are the sort for the young to read. Remember that. They are a great, an inestimable, and unspeakable means of improvement. Therefore, be careful in your selection, my young friends; be very careful; confine yourselves exclusively to Robertson's Sermons, Baxter's *Saint's Rest, The Innocents Abroad,* and works of that kind.

But I have said enough. I hope you will treasure up the instructions which I have given you, and make them a guide to your feet and a light to your understanding. Build your character thoughtfully and painstaking upon these precepts, and by and by, when you have got it built, you will be surprised and gratified to see how nicely and sharply it resembles everybody else's.

The Story of the Bad Little Boy

Once there was a bad little boy whose name was Jim—though, if you will notice, you will find that bad little boys are nearly always called James in your Sunday-school books. It was strange, but still it was true, that this one was called Jim.

He didn't have any sick mother, either—a sick mother who was pious and had the consumption, and would be glad to lie down in the grave and be at rest but for the strong love she bore her boy, and the anxiety she felt that the world might be harsh and cold toward him when she was gone. Most bad boys in the Sunday books are named James, and have sick mothers, who teach them to say, "Now I lay me down," etc., and sing them to sleep with sweet, plaintive voices, and then kiss them good night, and kneel down by the bedside and weep. But it was different with this fellow. He was named Jim, and there wasn't anything the matter with his mother—no consumption, nor anything of that kind. She was rather stout than otherwise, and she was not pious; moreover, she was not anxious on Jim's account. She said if he were to break his neck it wouldn't be much loss. She always spanked Jim to sleep, and she never kissed him good night; on the contrary, she boxed his ears when she was ready to leave him.

Once this little bad boy stole the key of the pantry, and slipped in there and helped himself to some jam, and filled up the vessel with tar, so that his mother would never know the difference; but all at once a terrible feeling didn't come over him, and something didn't seem whisper to him, "Is this right to disobey my mother? Isn't it sinful to do this? Where do bad little boys go who gobble up their good kind mother's jam?" and then he didn't kneel down all alone and promise never to be wicked any more, and rise up with a light, happy heart, and go and tell his mother all about it, and beg her forgiveness, and be blessed by her with tears of pride and thankfulness in her eyes. No; that is the way with all other bad boys in the books; but it happened otherwise with this Jim, strangely enough. He ate that jam, and said it was bully, in his sinful, vulgar way; and he put in the tar, and said that was bully also, and laughed, and observed "that the old woman would get up and snort" when she found it out; and when she did find it out, he denied knowing anything about it, and she whipped him severely, and he did the crying himself. Everything about this boy was curious—everything turned out differently with him from the way it does to the bad Jameses in the books.

Once he climbed up in Farmer Acorn's apple tree to steal apples, and the limb didn't break, and he didn't fall and break his arm, and get torn by the farmer's great dog, and then languish on a sickbed for weeks, and repent and become good. Oh, no; he stole as many apples as he wanted and came down all right; and he was ready for the dog, too, and knocked him endways with a brick when he came to tear him. It was very strange—nothing like it ever happened in those mild little books with marbled backs, and with pictures in them of men with swallow-tailed coats and bell-crowned hats, and pantaloons that are short in the legs, and women with the waists of their dresses under their arms, and no hoops on. Nothing like it in any of the Sunday-school books.

Once he stole the teacher's penknife, and, when he was

afraid it would be found out and he would get whipped, he slipped it into George Wilson's cap—poor Widow Wilson's son, the moral boy, the good little boy of the village, who always obeyed his mother, and never told an untruth, and was fond of his lessons, and infatuated with Sunday-school. And when the knife dropped from the cap, and poor George hung his head and blushed, as if in conscious guilt, and the grieved teacher charged the theft upon him, and was just in the very act of bringing the switch down upon his trembling shoulders, a white-haired, improbable justice of the peace did not suddenly appear in their midst, and strike an attitude and say, "Spare this noble boy—there stands the cowering culprit! I was passing the school door at recess, and, unseen myself, I saw the theft committed!" And then Jim didn't get whaled, and the venerable justice didn't read the tearful school a homily, and take George by the hand and say such a boy deserved to be exalted, and then tell him to come and make his home with him, and sweep out the office, and make fires, and run errands, and chop wood, and study law, and help his wife do household labors, and have all the balance of the time to play, and get forty cents a month and be happy. No; it would have happened that way in the books, but it didn't happen that way to Jim. No meddling old clam of a justice dropped in to make trouble, and so the model boy George got thrashed, and Jim was glad of it because, you know, Jim hated moral boys. Jim said he was "down on them milksops." Such was the coarse language of this bad, neglected boy.

But the strangest thing that ever happened to Jim was the time he went boating on Sunday, and didn't get drowned, and that other time that he got caught out in the storm when he was fishing on Sunday, and didn't get struck by lightning. Why, you might look, and look, all through the Sunday-school books from now till next Christmas, and you would never come across anything like this. Oh, no; you would find that all the bad boys who go boating on Sunday invariably get drowned; and all the bad boys who get caught out in storms when they are fishing on Sunday infallibly get struck by lightning. Boats with bad boys in them always upset on Sunday, and it always storms when bad boys go fishing on the Sabbath. How this Jim ever escaped is a mystery to me.

This Jim bore a charmed life—that must have been the way of it. He even gave the elephant in the menagerie a plug of tobacco, and the elephant didn't knock the top of his head off with his trunk. He browsed around the cupboard after essence of peppermint, and didn't make a mistake and drink *aqua fortis*. He stole his father's gun and went hunting on the Sabbath, and didn't shoot three or four of his fingers off. He struck his little sister on the temple with his fist when he was angry, and she didn't linger in pain through long summer days, and die with sweet words of forgiveness upon her lips that redoubled the anguish of his breaking heart. No; she got over it. He ran off and went to sea at last, and didn't come back and find himself sad and alone in the world, his loved ones sleeping in the quiet churchyard, and the vine-embowered home of his boyhood tumbled down and gone to decay. Ah, no; he came home as drunk as a piper, and got into the station-house the first thing.

And he grew up and married, and raised a large family, and brained them all with an ax one night, and got wealthy by all manner of cheating and rascality; and now he is the infernalest wickedest scoundrel in his native village, and is universally respected, and belongs to the legislature.

So you see, there never was a bad James in the Sunday-school books that had such a streak of luck as this sinful Jim with the charmed life.

The Story of the Good Little Boy

Once there was a good little boy by the name of Jacob Blivens. He always obeyed his parents, no matter how absurd and unreasonable their demands were; and he always learned his book, and never was late at Sabbath-school. He would not play hookey, even when his sober judgment told him it was the most profitable thing he could do. None of the other boys could ever make that boy out, he acted so strangely. He wouldn't lie, no matter how convenient it was. He just said it was wrong to lie, and that was sufficient for him. And he was so honest that he was simply ridiculous. The curious ways that that Jacob had, surpassed everything. He wouldn't play marbles on Sunday, he wouldn't rob birds' nests, he wouldn't give hot pennies to organ-grinders' monkeys; he didn't seem to take any interest in any kind of rational amusement. So the other boys used to try to reason it out and come to an understanding of him, but they couldn't arrive at any satisfactory conclusion. As I said before, they could only figure out a sort of vague idea that he was "afflicted," and so they took him under their protection, and never allowed any harm to come to him.

This good little boy read all the Sunday-school books; they were his greatest delight. This was the whole secret of it. He believed in the good little boys they put in the Sunday-school books; he had every confidence in them. He longed to come across one of them alive once; but he never did. They all died before his time, maybe. Whenever he read about a particularly good one he turned over quickly to the end to see what became of him, because he wanted to travel thousands of miles and gaze on him; but it wasn't any use; that good little boy always died in the last chapter, and there was a picture of the funeral, with all his relations and the Sunday-school children standing around the grave in pantaloons that were too short, and bonnets that were too large, and everybody crying into handkerchiefs that had as much as a yard and a half of stuff in them. He was always headed off in this way. He never could see one of those good little boys on account of his always dying in the last chapter.

Jacob had a noble ambition to be put in a Sunday-school book. He wanted to be put in, with pictures representing him gloriously declining to lie to his mother, and her weeping for joy about it; and pictures representing him standing on the doorstep giving a penny to a poor beggar-woman with six children, and telling her to spend it freely, but not to be extravagant, because extravagance is a sin; and pictures of him magnanimously refusing to tell on the bad boy who always lay in wait for him around the corner as he came from school, and welted him over the head with a lath, and then chased him home saying "Hi! hi!" as he proceeded. That was the ambition of young Jacob Blivens. He wished to be put in a Sunday-school book. It made him feel a little uncomfortable sometimes when he reflected that the good little boys always died. He loved to live, you know, and this was the most unpleasant feature about being a Sunday-school-book boy. He knew it was not healthy to be good. He knew it was more fatal than consumption to be so supernaturally good as the boys in the books were; he knew that none of them had ever been able to stand it long, and it pained him to think that if they put him in a book he wouldn't ever see it, or even if they did get the book out before he died it wouldn't be popular without any picture of his funeral in the back part of it. It couldn't be much of a Sunday-school book that couldn't tell about the advice he gave to the community when he was dying. So at last, of course, he had made up his mind to do the best he could under the circumstances—to live right, and hang on as long as he could, and have his dying speech all ready when his time came.

But somehow nothing ever went right with the good little boy; nothing ever turned out with him the way it turned out with the good little boys in the books. They always had a good time, and the bad boys had broken legs; but in his case there was a screw loose somewhere, and it all happened just the other way. When he found Jim Blake stealing apples, and went under the tree to read to him about the bad little boy who fell out of a neighbor's tree and broke his arm, Jim fell out of the tree, too, but he fell on *him* and broke *his* arm, and Jim wasn't hurt at all. Jacob couldn't understand that. There wasn't anything in the books like it.

And once, when some bad boys pushed a blind man over in the mud, and Jacob ran to help him up and receive his blessing, the blind man did not give him any blessing at all, but whacked him over the head with his stick and said he would like to catch him shoving *him* again, and then pretending to help him up. This was not in accordance with any of the books. Jacob looked them all over to see.

One thing that Jacob wanted to do was find a lame dog that hadn't any place to stay, and was hungry and persecuted, and bring him home and pet him and have that dog's imperishable gratitude. And at last he found one and was happy; and he brought him home and fed him, but when he was going to pet him the dog flew at him and tore all the clothes off him except for those that were in front, and made a spectacle of him that was astonishing. He examined authorities, but he could not understand the matter. It was of the same breed of dogs that was in the books, but it acted very differently. Whatever this boy did he got into trouble. The very things the boys in the books got rewarded for turned out to be the most unprofitable things he could invest in.

Once, when we was on his way to Sunday-school, he saw some bad boys starting off pleasuring in a sailboat. He was filled with consternation, because he knew from his reading that boys who went sailing on Sunday invariably got drowned. So he ran out on a raft to warn them, but a log turned with him and slid him into the river. A man got him out pretty soon, and the doctor pumped the water out of him, and gave him a fresh start with his bellows, but he caught cold and lay sick abed nine weeks. But the most unaccountable thing about it was that the bad boys in the boat had a good time all day, and then reached home alive and well in the most surprising manner. Jacob Blivens said there was nothing like these things in the books. He was perfectly dumbfounded.

When he got well he was a little discouraged, but he resolved to keep on trying anyhow. He knew that so far his experiences wouldn't do to go in a book, but he hadn't yet reached the allotted term of life for good little boys, and he hoped to be able to make up a record yet if he could hold on till his time was fully up. If everything else failed he had his dying speech to fall back on.

He examined his authorities, and found it was now time for him to go to sea as a cabin-boy. He called on a ship-captain and made his application, and when the captain asked for his recommendations he proudly drew out a tract and pointed to the word, "To Jacob Blivens, from his affectionate teacher." But the captain was a coarse, vulgar man, and he said, "Oh, that be blowed! *that* wasn't any proof that he knew how to wash dishes or handle a slush-bucket, and he guessed he didn't want him." This was altogether the most extraordinary thing that ever happened to Jacob in all his life. A compliment from a teacher, on a tract, had never failed to move the tenderest emotions of ship-captains, and open the way to all offices of honor and profit in their gift— it never had in any book that ever *he* had read. He could hardly believe his senses.

This boy always had a hard time of it. Nothing ever came out according to the authorities with him. At last, one day, when he was around hunting up little bad boys to admonish, he found a lot of them in the old iron-foundry fixing up a little joke on fourteen or fifteen dogs, which they had tied together in long procession, and were going to ornament with empty nitroglycerin cans made fast to their tails. Jacob's heart was touched. He sat down on one of those cans (for he never minded grease when duty was before him), and he took hold of the foremost dog by the collar, and turned his reproving eye upon wicked Tom Jones. But just at that moment Alderman McWelter, full of wrath, stepped in. All the bad boys ran away, but Jacob Blivens rose in conscious innocence and began one of those stately little Sunday-school-book speeches which always commence with "Oh, sir!" in dead opposition to the fact that no boy, good or bad, ever starts a remark with "Oh, sir." But the alderman never waited to hear the rest. He took Jacob Blivens by the ear and turned him around, and hit him with a whack in the rear with the flat of his hand; and in an instant the good little boy shot out through the roof and soared away toward the sun, with the fragments of those fifteen dogs stringing after him like the tail of a kite. And there wasn't a sign of that alderman or that old iron-foundry left on the face of the earth; and, as for young Jacob Blivens, he never got a chance to make his last dying speech after all his trouble fixing it up, unless he made it to the birds; because, although the bulk of him came down all right in a tree-top in an adjoining county, the rest of him was apportioned around among four townships, and so they had to hold five inquests on him to find out whether he was dead or not, and how it occurred. You never saw a boy scattered so.*

Thus perished the good little boy who did the best he could, but didn't come out according to the books. Every boy who ever did as he did prospered except him. His case is truly remarkable. It will probably never be accounted for.

---

*This glycerin catastrophe is borrowed from a floating newspaper item, whose author's name I would give if I knew it.

Girls

In my capacity of publisher I recently received a manuscript from a teacher which embodied a number of answers given by her pupils to questions propounded. These answers show that the children had nothing but the sound to go by—the sense was perfectly empty. Here are some of their answers to words they were asked to define: Auriferous—pertaining to an orifice; ammonia—the food of the gods; equestrian—one who asks questions; parasite—a kind of umbrella; ipecac—a man who likes a good dinner. And here is the definition of an ancient word honored by a great party: Republican—a sinner mentioned in the Bible. And here is an innocent deliverance of a zoological kind: "There are a good many donkeys in the theological gardens." Here also is a definition which really isn't very bad in its way: Demagogue—a vessel containing beer and other liquids. Here, too, is a sample of a boy's composition on girls, which I must say, I rather like:

"Girls are very stuckup and dignified in their manner and behaveyour. They think more of dress than anything and like to play with dowls and rags. They cry if they see a cow in a far distance and are afraid of guns. They stay at home all the time and go to church every Sunday. They are al-ways sick. They are al-ways funy and making fun of boys hands and they say how dirty. They cant play marbles. I pity them poor things. They make fun of boys and then turn round and love them. I don't belave they ever kiled a cat or anything. They look out every nite and say, 'Oh, a'nt the moon lovely!' Thir is one thing I have not told and that is they al-ways now their lessons bettern boys."

The Babies

I like that. We have not all had the good fortune to be ladies. We have not all been generals, or poets, or statesmen; but when the toast works down to the babies, we stand on common ground. It is a shame that for a thousand years the world's banquets have utterly ignored the baby, as if he didn't amount to anything. If you will stop and think a minute—if you will go back fifty or one hundred years to your early married life and recontemplate your first baby—you will remember that he amounted to a good deal, and even something over. You soldiers all know that when that little fellow arrived at family headquarters you had to hand in your resignation. He took entire command. You became his lackey, his mere body-servant, and you had to stand around too. He was not a commander who made allowances for time, distance, weather, or anything else. You had to execute his order whether it was possible or not. And there was only one form of marching in his manual of tactics, and that was the double-quick. He treated you with every sort of insolence and disrespect, and the bravest of you didn't dare to say a word. You could face the death-storm at Donelson and Vicksburg, and give back blow for blow; but when he clawed your whiskers, and pulled your hair, and twisted your nose, you had to take it. When the thunders of war were sounding in your ears you set your faces toward the batteries, and advanced with steady tread; but when he turned on the terrors of his war-whoop you advanced in the other direction, and mighty glad of the chance, too. When he called for soothing-syrup, did you venture to throw out any side-remarks about certain services being unbecoming an officer and a gentleman? No. You got up and *got* it. When he ordered his pap bottle and it was not warm, did you talk back? Not you. You went to work and *warmed* it. You even descended so far in your menial office as to take a suck at that warm, insipid stuff yourself, to see if it was right—three parts water to one of milk, a touch of sugar to modify the colic, and a drop of peppermint to kill those immortal hiccoughs. I can taste the stuff yet. And how many things you learned as you went along! Sentimental young folks still take stock in that beautiful old saying that when the baby smiles in his sleep, it is because the angels are whispering to him. Very pretty, but too thin—simply wind on the stomach, my friends. If the baby proposed to take a walk at his usual hour, two o'clock in the morning, didn't you rise up promptly and remark, with a mental addition which would not improve a Sunday-school book *much,* that that was the very thing you were about to propose yourself? Oh! you were under good discipline, and as you went fluttering up and down the room in your undress uniform, you not only prattled undignified baby-talk, but even tuned up your martial voices and tried to *sing!*—*Rock-a-by Baby in the Tree-top,* for instance. What a spectacle for an Army of the Tennessee! And what an affliction for the neighbors, too; for it is not everybody within a mile around that likes military music at three in the morning. And when you had been keeping this sort of thing up two or three hours, and your little velvet-head intimated that nothing suited him like exercise and noise, what did you do? You simply *went* on until you dropped in the last ditch. The idea that a *baby* doesn't *amount* to anything! Why, *one* baby is just a house and a front yard full by itself. *One* baby can furnish more business than you and your whole Interior Department can attend to. He is enterprising, irrepressible, brimful of lawless activities. Do what you please, you can't make him stay on the reservation. Sufficient unto the day is one baby. As long as you are in your right mind don't you ever pray for twins. Twins amount to a permanent riot. And there ain't any real difference between triplets and an insurrection.

Yes, it was high time for a toast-master to recognize the importance of the babies. Think what is in store for the present crop! Fifty years from now we shall all be dead, I trust, and then this flag, if it still survive (and let us hope it may), will be floating over a Republic numbering 200,000,000 souls, according to the settled laws of our increase. Our present schooner of State will have grown into a political leviathan—a *Great Eastern*. The cradled babies of to-day will be on deck. Let them be well trained, for we are going to leave a big contract on their hands. Among the three or four million cradles now rocking in the land are some which this nation would preserve for ages as sacred things, if we could know which ones they are. In one of these cradles the unconscious Farragut of the future is at this moment teething—think of it!—and putting in a world of dead earnest, unarticulated, but perfectly justifiable profanity over it, too. In another the future renowned astronomer is blinking at the shining Milky Way with but a languid interest—poor little chap!—and wondering what has become of that other one they call the wet-nurse. In another the future great historian is lying—and doubtless will continue to lie until his earthly mission is ended. In another the future President is busying himself with no profounder problem of state than what the mischief has become of his hair so early; and in a mighty array of other cradles there are now some 60,000 future office-seekers, getting ready to furnish him occasion to grapple with that same old problem a second time. And in still one more cradle, somewhere under the flag, the future illustrious commander-in-chief of the American armies is so little burdened with his approaching grandeurs and responsibilities as to be giving his whole strategic mind at this moment to trying to find out some way to get his big toe into his mouth—an achievement which, meaning no disrespect, the illustrious guest of this evening* turned *his* entire attention to some fifty-six years ago; and if the child is but a prophecy of the man, there are mighty few who will doubt that he *succeeded.*

*Ulysses S. Grant—Ed.

III.

THE HUMAN CONDITION

Conclusion

OLD MAN. You have been taking a holiday?
YOUNG MAN. Yes; a mountain-tramp covering a week. Are you ready to talk?
O.M. Quite ready. What shall we begin with?
Y.M. Well, lying abed resting-up, two days and nights, I have thought over all these talks, and passed them carefully in review. With this result: that. . . . that. . . . are you intending to publish your notions about Man some day?
O.M. Now and then, in these past twenty years, the Master inside of me has half-intended to order me to set them to paper and publish them. Do I have to tell you why the order has remained unissued, or can you explain such a simple thing without my help?
Y.M. By your doctrine, it is simplicity itself: outside influences moved your interior Master to give the order; stronger outside influences deterred him. Without the outside influences, neither of these impulses could ever have been born, since a person's brain is incapable of originating an idea within itself.
O.M. Correct. Go on.
Y.M. The matter of publishing or withholding is still in your Master's hands. If, some day, an outside influence shall determine him to publish, he will give the order, and it will be obeyed.
O.M. That is correct. Well?
Y.M. Upon reflection I have arrived at the conviction that

the publication of your doctrines would be harmful. Do you pardon me?

O.M. Pardon *you*? You have done nothing. You are an instrument—a speaking-trumpet. Speaking-trumpets are not responsible for what is said through them. Outside influences—in the form of life-long teachings, trainings, notions, prejudices, and other second-hand importations—have persuaded the Master within you that the publication of these doctrines would be harmful. Very well, this is quite natural, and was to be expected; in fact was inevitable. Go on; for the sake of ease and convenience, stick to habit: speak in the first person, and tell me what your Master thinks about it.

Y.M. Well, to begin: it is a desolating doctrine; it is not inspiring, enthusing, uplifting. It takes the glory out of a man, it takes the pride out of him, it takes the heroism out of him, it denies him all personal credit, all applause; it not only degrades him to a machine, but allows him no control over the machine; makes a mere coffee-mill of him, and neither permits him to supply the coffee nor turn the crank; his sole and piteously humble function being to grind coarse or fine, according to his make, outside impulses doing all the rest.

O.M. It is correctly stated. Tell me—what do men admire most in each other?

Y.M. Intellect, courage, majesty of build, beauty of countenance, charity, benevolence, magnanimity, kindliness, heroism, and—and—

O.M. I would not go any further. These are *elementals*. Virtue, fortitude, holiness, truthfulness, loyalty, high ideals—these, and all the related qualities that are named in the dictionary, are *made out of the elementals*, by blendings, combinations, and shadings of the elementals, just as one makes green by blending blue and yellow, and makes several shades and tints of red by modifying the elemental red.

Conclusion

There are seven elemental colors, they are all in the rainbow, out of them we manufacture and name fifty shades of them. You have named the elementals of the human rainbow, and also one *blend*—heroism, which is made out of courage and magnanimity. Very well, then; which of these elements does the possessor of it manufacture for himself? Is it intellect?

Y.M. No

O.M. Why?

Y.M. He is born with it.

O.M. Is it courage?

Y.M. No. He is born with it.

O.M. Is it majesty of build, beauty of countenance?

Y.M. No. They are birthrights.

O.M. Take those others—the elemental moral qualities—charity, benevolence, magnanimity, kindliness; fruitful seeds, out of which spring, through cultivation by outside influences, all the manifold blends and combinations of virtues named in the dictionaries: does man manufacture any one of those seeds, or are they all born in him?

Y.M. Born in him.

O.M. Who manufactures them, then?

Y.M. God.

O.M. Where does the credit of it belong?

Y.M. To God.

O.M. And the glory of which you spoke, and the applause?

Y.M. To God.

O.M.. Then it is *you* who degrade man. You make him claim glory, praise, flattery, for every valuable thing he possesses—*borrowed* finery, the whole of it; no rag of it earned by himself, not a detail of it produced by his own labor. *You* make man a humbug; have I done worse by him?

Y.M. You have made a machine of him.

O.M. Who devised that cunning and beautiful mechanism, a man's hand?

Y.M. God.

O.M. Who devised the law by which it automatically hammers out of a piano an elaborate piece of music, without error, while the man is thinking about something else, or talking to a friend?

Y.M. God.

O.M. Who devised the blood? Who devised the wonderful machinery which automatically drives its renewing and refreshing streams through the body, day and night, without assistance or advice from the man? Who devised the man's mind, whose machinery works automatically, interests itself in what it pleases, regardless of his will or desire, labors all night when it likes, deaf to his appeals for mercy? God devised all these things. I have not made man a machine, God made him a machine. I am merely calling attention to the fact, nothing more. Is it wrong to call attention to a fact? Is it a crime?

Y.M. I think it is wrong to *expose* a fact when harm can come of it.

O.M. Go on.

Y.M. Look at the matter as it stands now. Man has been taught that he is the supreme marvel of the Creation; he believes it; in all ages he has never doubted it, whether he was a naked savage, or clothed in purple and fine linen, and civilized. This has made his heart buoyant, his life cheery. His pride in himself, his sincere admiration of himself, his joy in what he supposed were his own and unassisted achievements, and his exultation over the praise and applause which they evoked—these have exalted him, enthused him, ambitioned him to higher and higher flights; in a word, made his life worth the living. But by your scheme, all this is abolished: he is degraded to a machine, he is a nobody, his noble prides wither to mere vanities; let him strive as he may, he can never be any better than his humblest and stupidest neighbor; he would never be cheerful again, his life would not be worth the living.

O.M. You really think that?

Y.M. I certainly do.

O.M. Have you ever seen me uncheerful, unhappy?

Y.M. No.

O.M. Well, *I* believe these things. Why have they not made me unhappy?

Y.M. Oh, well—temperament, of course! You never let *that* escape from your scheme.

O.M. That is correct. If a man is born with an unhappy temperament, nothing can make him happy; if he is born with a happy temperament, nothing can make him unhappy.

Y.M. What—not even a degrading and heart-chilling system of beliefs?

O.M. Beliefs? Mere beliefs? Mere convictions? They are powerless. They strive in vain against inborn temperament.

Y.M. I can't believe that, and I don't.

O.M. Now you are speaking hastily. It shows that you have not studiously examined the facts. Of all your intimates, which one is the happiest? Isn't it Burgess?

Y.M. Easily.

O.M. And which one is the unhappiest? Henry Adams?

Y.M. Without a question!

O.M. I know them well. They are extremes, abnormals; their temperaments are as opposite as the poles. Their life-histories are about alike—but look at the results! Their ages are about the same—around about fifty. Burgess has always been buoyant, hopeful, happy; Adams has always been cheerless, hopeless, despondent. As young fellows, both tried country journalism—and failed. Burgess didn't seem to mind it; Adams couldn't smile, he could only mourn and groan over what happened, and torture himself with vain regrets for not having done so-and-so instead of so-and-so—*then* he would have succeeded. They tried the law—and failed. Burgess remained happy—because he couldn't help it, Adams was wretched—because he couldn't help it. From that day to this, those two men have gone on trying things and failing: Burgess has come out happy and cheerful every time, Adams the reverse. Now we do absolutely know that these men's inborn temperaments have remained unchanged through all the vicissitudes of their material affairs. Let us see how it is with their immaterialities. Both have been zealous democrats; both have been zealous republicans; both have been zealous mugwumps. Burgess has always found happiness and Adams unhappiness, in these several political beliefs and their migrations out of them. Both of these men have been Presbyterians, Universalists, Methodists, Catholics,—then Presbyterians again, then Methodists again. Burgess has always found rest in these excursions, and Adams unrest; they are trying Christian Science, now, with the customary result, the inevitable result. No political or religious belief can make Burgess unhappy or the other man happy. I assure you it is purely a matter of temperament. Beliefs are *acquirements*, temperaments are *born*; beliefs are subject to change, nothing whatever can change temperament.

Y.M. You have instanced extreme temperaments.

O.M. Yes. The half dozen others are modifications of the extremes. But the law is the same. Where the temperament is two-thirds happy, or two-thirds unhappy, no political or religious beliefs can change the proportions. The vast majority of temperaments are pretty equally balanced; the intensities are absent, and this enables a nation to learn to accommodate itself to its political and religious circum-

CONCLUSION

stances and like them, be satisfied with them, at last prefer them. Nations do not *think,* they only *feel.* They get their feelings at second-hand—through their temperaments, not their brains. A nation can be brought—by force of circumstances, not argument—to reconcile itself to *any kind of government or religion that can be devised;* in time it will fit itself to the required conditions; later, it will prefer them; and will fiercely fight for them. As instances, you have all history: the Greeks, the Romans, the Persians, the Egyptians, the Russians, the Germans, the French, the English, the Spaniards, the Americans, the South Americans, the Japanese, the Chinese, the Hindoos, the Turks—a thousand wild and tame religions, every kind of government that can be thought of, from tiger to housecat, each nation *knowing* it has the only true religion and the only sane system of government, each despising all the others, each an ass and not suspecting it, each proud of its fancied supremacy, each perfectly sure it is the pet of God, each with undoubting confidence summoning Him to take command in time of war, each surprised when He goes over to the enemy, but by habit able to excuse it and resume compliments—in a word, the whole human race content, always content, persistently content, indestructibly content, happy, thankful, proud, *no matter what its religion is, nor whether its master be tiger or housecat.* Am I stating facts? You know I am. Is the human race cheerful? You know it is. Considering what it can stand, and be happy, you do me too much honor when you think that *I* can place before it a system of plain cold facts that can take the cheerfulness out of it. Nothing can do that. Everything has been tried. Without success. I beg you not to be troubled.

The Ladies

I am proud, indeed, of the distinction of being chosen to respond to this especial toast, to "The Ladies," or to women if you please, for that is the preferable term, perhaps; it is certainly the older and therefore the more entitled to reverence. I have noticed that the Bible, with that plain, blunt honesty which is such a conspicuous characteristic of the Scriptures, is always particular never to refer to even the illustrious mother of all mankind as a "lady," but speaks of her as a woman. It is odd, but you will find it is so. I am peculiarly proud of this honor, because I think that the toast to women is one which, by right and by every rule of gallantry, should take precedence of all others—of the army, of the navy, of even royalty itself—perhaps, though the latter is not necessary in this day and in this land, for the reason that, tacitly, you do drink a broad general health to all good women when you drink the health of the Queen of England and the Princess of Wales. I have in mind a poem just now which is familiar to you all, familiar to everybody. And what an inspiration that was, and how instantly the present toast recalls the verses to all our minds when the most noble, the most gracious, the purest, the sweetest of all poets says:

> "Woman! O woman!——er——
> Wom——"

However, you remember the lines; and you remember how feelingly, how daintily, how almost imperceptibly the verses raise up before you, feature by feature, the idea of a true and perfect woman; and how, as you contemplate the finished marvel, your homage grows into worship of the intellect that could create so fair a thing out of mere breath, mere words. And you call to mind now, as I speak, how the poet, with stern fidelity to the history of all humanity, delivers this beautiful child of his heart and his brain over to the trials and sorrows that must come to all, sooner or later, that abide in the earth, and how the pathetic story culminates in that apostrophe—so wild, so regretful, so full of mournful retrospection. The lines run thus:

> "*Alas!—alas!—a—alas!*
> ——*Alas!* ————*alas!*"

—and so on. I do not remember the rest; but, taken together, it seems to me that poem is the noblest tribute to woman that human genius has ever brought forth—and I feel that if I were to talk hours I could not do my great theme completer or more graceful justice than I have now done in simply quoting that poet's matchless words. The phases of the womanly nature are infinite in their variety. Take any type of woman, and you shall find in it something to respect, something to admire, something to love. And you shall find the whole joining you heart and hand. Who was more patriotic than Joan of Arc? Who was braver? Who has given us a grander instance of self-sacrificing devotion? Ah! you remember, you remember well, what a throb of pain, what a great tidal wave of grief swept over us all when Joan of Arc fell at Waterloo. Who does not sorrow for the loss of Sappho, the sweet singer of Israel? Who among us does not miss the gentle ministrations, the softening influences, the humble piety of Lucretia Borgia? Who can join in the heartless libel that says woman is extravagant in dress when he can look back and call to mind our simple and lowly mother Eve arrayed in her modification of the Highland costume? Sir, women have been soldiers, women have been painters, women have been poets. As long as language lives the name of Cleopatra will live. And not because she conquered George III.—but because she wrote these divine lines:

> *"Let dogs delight to bark and bite,*
> *For God hath made them so."*

The story of the world is adorned with the names of illustrious ones of our own sex—some of them sons of St. Andrew, too—Scott, Bruce, Burns, the warrior Wallace, Ben Nevis—the gifted Ben Lomond, and the great new Scotchman, Ben Disraeli. Out of the great plains of history tower whole mountain ranges of sublime women—the Queen of Sheba, Josephine, Semiramis, Sairey Gamp; the list is endless—but I will not call the mighty roll, the names rise up in your own memories at the mere suggestion, luminous with the glory of deeds that cannot die, hallowed by the loving worship of the good and the true of all epochs and all climes. Suffice it for our pride and our honor that we in our day have added to it such names as those of Grace Darling and Florence Nightingale. Woman is all that she should be—gentle, patient, longsuffering, trustful, unselfish, full of generous impulses. It is her blessed mission to comfort the sorrowing, plead for the erring, encourage the faint of purpose, succor the distressed, uplift the fallen, befriend the friendless—in a word, afford the healing of her sympathies and a home in her heart for all the bruised and persecuted children of misfortune that knock at its hospitable door. And when I say, God bless her, there is none among us who has known the ennobling affection of a wife, or the steadfast devotion of a mother but in his heart will say, Amen!

The Five Boons of Life

I

In the morning of life came the good fairy with her basket, and said:

"Here are gifts. Take one, leave the others. And be wary, choose wisely; oh, choose wisely! for only one of them is valuable."

The gifts were five: Fame, Love, Riches, Pleasure, Death. The youth said, eagerly:

"There is no need to consider"; and he chose Pleasure.

He went out into the world and sought out the pleasures that youth delights in. But each in its turn was short-lived and disappointing, vain and empty; and each, departing, mocked him. In the end he said: "These years I have wasted. If I could but choose again, I would choose wisely."

II

The fairy appeared, and said:

"Four of the gifts remain. Choose once more; and oh, remember—time is flying, and only one of them is precious."

The man considered long, and then chose Love; and did not mark the tears that rose in the fairy's eyes.

After many, many years the man sat by a coffin, in an empty home. And he communed with himself, saying: "One by one they have gone away and left me; and now she lies here, the dearest and the last. Desolation after desolation has swept over me; for each hour of happiness the treacherous trader, Love, had sold me I have paid a thousand hours of grief. Out of my heart of hearts I curse him."

III

"Choose again." It was the fairy speaking.
"The years have taught you wisdom—surely it must be so. Three gifts remain. Only one of them has any worth—remember it, and choose warily."
The man reflected long, then chose Fame; and the fairy, sighing, went her way.
Years went by and she came again, and stood behind the man where he sat solitary in the fading day, thinking. And she knew his thought:
"My name filled the world, and its praises were on every tongue, and it seemed well with me for a little while. How little a while it was! Then came envy; then detraction; then calumny; then hate; then persecution. Then derision, which is the beginning of the end. And last of all came pity, which is the funeral of fame. Oh, the bitterness and misery of renown! target for mud in its prime, for contempt and compassion in its decay."

IV

"Choose yet again." It was the fairy's voice. "Two gifts remain. And do not despair. In the beginning there was but one that was precious, and it is still here."
"Wealth—which is power! How blind I was!" said the man. "Now, at last, life will be worth the living. I will spend, squander, dazzle. These mockers and despisers will crawl in the dirt before me, and I will feed my hungry heart

with their envy. I will have all luxuries, all joys, all enchantments of the spirit, all contentments of the body that man holds dear. I will buy, buy, buy! deference, respect, esteem, worship—every pinchbeck grace of life the market of a trivial world can furnish forth. I have lost much time, and chosen badly heretofore, but let that pass; I was ignorant then, and could but take for best what seemed so."

Three short years went by, and a day came when the old man sat shivering in a mean garret; and he was gaunt and wan and hollow-eyed, and clothed in rags; and he was gnawing a dry crust and mumbling:

"Curse all the world's gifts, for mockeries and gilded lies! And miscalled, every one. They are not gifts, but merely lendings. Pleasure, Love, Fame, Riches: they are but temporary disguises for lasting realities—Pain, Grief, Shame, Poverty. The fairy said true; all in her store there was but one gift which was precious, only one that was not valueless. How poor and cheap and mean I know those others now to be, compared with that inestimable one, that dear and sweet and kindly one, that steeps in dreamless and enduring sleep the pains that persecute the body, and the shames and griefs that eat the mind and heart. Bring it! I am weary, I would rest."

V

The fairy came, bringing again four of the gifts, but Death was wanting. She said:

"I gave it to a mother's pet, a little child. It was ignorant, but trusted me, asking me to choose for it. You did not ask me to choose."

"Oh, miserable me! What is there left for me?"

"What not even you have deserved: the wanton insult of Old Age."

The Turning Point of My Life

I

If I understand the idea, the *Bazar* invites several of us to write upon the above text. It means the change in my life's course which introduced what must be regarded by me as the most *important* condition of my career. But it also implies—without intention, perhaps—that that turning point was *itself*, individually, the creator of the new condition. This gives it too much distinction, too much prominence, too much credit. It is only the *last* link in a very long chain of turning points commissioned to produce the weighty result; it is not any more important than the humblest of its ten thousand predecessors. Each of the ten thousand did its appointed share, on its appointed date, in forwarding the scheme, and they were all necessary; to have left out any one of them would have defeated the scheme and brought about *some other* result. I know we have a fashion of saying "such and such an event was *the* turning point in my life," but we shouldn't say it. We should merely grant that its place as *last* link in the chain makes it the most *conspicuous* link; in real importance it has no advantage over any one of its predecessors.

Perhaps the most celebrated turning point recorded in history was the crossing of the Rubicon. Suetonius says:

> Coming up with his troops on the banks of the Rubicon, he halted for a while, and, revolving in his

mind the importance of the step he was on the point of taking, he turned to those about him and said, "We may still retreat; but if we pass this little bridge, nothing is left for us but to fight it out in arms."

This was a stupendously important moment. And all the incidents, big and little, of Caesar's previous life had been leading up to it, stage by stage, link by link. This was the *last* link—merely the last one, and no bigger than the others; but as we gaze back at it through the inflating mists of our imagination, it looks as big as the orbit of Neptune.

You, the reader, have a *personal* interest in that link, and so have I; so has the rest of the human race. It was one of the links in your life-chain, and it was one of the links in mine. We may wait, now, with bated breath, while Caesar reflects. Your fate and mine are involved in his decision.

While he was thus hesitating, the following incident occurred. A person remarkable for his noble mien and graceful aspect, appeared close at hand, sitting and playing upon a pipe. When not only the shepherds, but a number of soldiers also, flocked to listen to him, and some trumpeters among them, he snatched a trumpet from one of them, ran to the river with it, and sounding the advance with a piercing blast, crossed to the other side. Upon this, Caesar exclaimed, "Let us go whither the omens of the gods and the iniquity of our enemies call us. *The die is cast."*

So he crossed—and changed the future of the whole human race, for all time. But that stranger was a link in Caesar's life-chain, too; and a necessary one. We don't know his name, we never hear of him again, he was very casual, he acts like an accident; but he was no accident, he was there by compulsion of *his* life-chain, to blow the electrifying blast that was to make up Caesar's mind for him, and thence go piping down the aisles of history forever.

If the stranger hadn't been there! But he *was*. And Caesar crossed. With such results! Such vast events—each a link in the *human race's* life-chain; each event producing the next one, and that one the next one, and so on: the destruction of the republic; the founding of the empire; the breaking up of the empire; the rise of Christianity upon its ruins; the spread of the religion to other lands—and so on: link by link took its appointed place at its appointed time, the discovery of America being one of them; our Revolution another; the inflow of English and other immigrants another; their drift westward (my ancestors among them) another; the settlement of certain of them in Missouri—which resulted in *me*. For I was one of the unavoidable results of the crossing of the Rubicon. If the stranger, with his trumpet blast, had stayed away (which he *couldn't*, for he was an appointed link), Caesar would not have crossed. What would have happened, in that case, we can never guess. We only know that the thing that did happen would not have happened. They might have been replaced by equally prodigious things, of course, but their nature and results are beyond our guessing. But the matter that interests me personally is, that I would not be *here,* now, but somewhere else; and probably black—there is no telling. Very well, I am glad he crossed. And very really and thankfully glad, too, though I never cared anything about it before.

II

To me, the most important feature of my life is its literary feature. I have been professionally literary something more than forty years. There have been many turning points in my life, but the one that was the last link in the chain appointed to conduct me to the literary guild is the most *conspicuous* link in that chain. *Because* it was the last one. It was not any more important than its predecessors. All the other links have an inconspicuous look, except the crossing of the Rubicon; but as factors in making me literary they are all of the one size, the crossing of the Rubicon included.

I know how I came to be literary, and I will tell the steps that led up to it and brought it about.

The crossing of the Rubicon was not the first one, it was hardly even a recent one; I should have to go back ages before Caesar's day to find the first one. To save space I will go back only a couple of generations, and start with an incident of my boyhood. When I was twelve and a half years old, my father died. It was in the spring. The summer came, and brought with it an epidemic of measles. For a time, a child died almost every day. The village was paralysed with fright, distress, despair. Children that were not smitten with the disease were imprisoned in their homes to save them from the infection. In the homes there were no cheerful faces, there was no music, there was no singing but of solemn hymns, no voice but of prayer, no romping was allowed, no noise, no laughter, the family moved spectrally about on tiptoe, in a ghostly hush. I was a prisoner. My soul was steeped in this awful dreariness—and in fear. At some time or other every day and every night a sudden shiver shook me to the marrow, and I said to myself, "There, I've got it! and I shall die." Life on those miserable terms was not worth living, and at last I made up my mind to get the disease and have it over, one way or the other. I escaped from the house and went to the house of a neighbor where a playmate of mine was very ill with the malady. When the chance offered I crept in his room and got into bed with him. I was discovered by his mother and sent back into captivity. But I had the disease; they could not take that from me. I came near to dying. The whole village was interested, and anxious, and sent for news of me every day; and not only once a day, but several times. Everybody believed I would die; but on the fourteenth day a change came for the worse and they were disappointed.

This was a turning point in my life. (Link number one.) For when I got well my mother closed my school career and apprenticed me to a printer. She was tired of trying to keep me out of mischief, and the adventure of the measles decided her to put me into more masterful hands than hers.

I became a printer, and began to add one link after another to the chain which was to lead me into the literary profession. A long road, but I could not know that; and as I did not know what its goal was, or even that it had one, I was indifferent. Also contented.

A young printer wanders around a good deal, seeking and finding work; and seeking again, when necessity commands. N.B. Necessity is a *Circumstance;* Circumstance is man's master—and when Circumstance commands, he must obey; he may argue the matter—that is his privilege, just as it is the honorable privilege of a falling body to argue with the attraction of gravitation—but it won't do any good, he must *obey.* I wandered for ten years, under the guidance and dictatorship of Circumstance, and finally arrived in a city of Iowa, where I worked several months. Among the books that interested me in those days was one about the Amazon. The traveler told an alluring tale of his long voyage up the great river from Para to the sources of the Madiera, through the heart of an enchanted land, a land wastefully rich in tropical wonders, a romantic land where all the birds and flowers and animals were of the museum varieties, and where the alligator and the crocodile and the monkey seemed as much at home as if they were in the Zoo. Also, he told an astonishing tale about *coca,* a vegetable product of miraculous powers; asserting that it was so nourishing and so strength-giving that the native of the mountains of the Madiera region would tramp up-hill and down all day on a pinch of powdered coca and require no other sustenance.

I was fired with a longing to ascend the Amazon. Also with a longing to open up a trade in coca with all the world. During months I dreamed that dream, and tried to contrive ways to get to Para and spring that splendid enterprise upon an unsuspecting planet. But all in vain. A person may *plan* as much as he wants to, but nothing of consequence is likely to come of it until the magician *Circumstance* steps in and takes the matter off his hands. At last Circumstance came to my help. It was in this way. Circumstance, to help or hurt another man, made him lose a fifty-dollar bill in the street; and to help or hurt me, made me find it. I advertised the find, and left for the Amazon the same day. This was another turning point, another link.

Could Circumstance have ordered up another dweller in that town to go to the Amazon and open up a world-trade in coca on a fifty-dollar basis and been obeyed? No, I was the only one. There were other fools there—shoals and shoals of them—but they were not of my kind. I was the only one of my kind.

Circumstance is powerful, but it cannot work alone, it has to have a partner. Its partner is man's *temperament*—his natural disposition. His temperament is not his invention, it is *born* in him, and he has no authority over it, neither is he responsible for its acts. He cannot change it, nothing can change it, nothing can modify it,—except temporarily. But it won't stay modified. It is permanent; like the color of the man's eyes and the shape of his ears. Blue eyes are gray, in certain unusual lights; but they resume their natural color when that stress is removed.

A Circumstance that will coerce one man, will have no effect upon a man of a different temperament. If Circumstance had thrown the bank note in Caesar's way, his temperament would not have made him start for the Amazon. His temperament would have compelled him to do something with the money, but not that. It might have made him advertise the note—and *wait*. We can't tell. Also, it might have made him go to New York and buy into the government; with results that would leave Tweed nothing to learn when it came his turn.

Very well, Circumstance furnished the capital, and my temperament told me what to do with it. Sometimes a temperament is an ass. When that is the case the owner of it is an ass, too, and is going to remain one. Training, experience, association, can temporarily so elevate him that people will think he is a mule, but they will be mistaken. Artificially he *is* a mule, for the time being, but at bottom he is an ass yet, and will remain one.

By temperament I was the kind of person that *does* things. Does them, and reflects afterward. So I started for the Amazon, without reflecting, and without asking any questions. That was more than fifty years ago. In all that time my temperament has not changed, by even a shade. I have been punished many and many a time, and bitterly, for doing things first and reflecting afterward, but these tortures have been of no value to me; I still do the thing commanded by Circumstance and Temperament, and reflect afterward. Always violently. When I am reflecting, on those occasions, even deaf persons can hear me think.

I went by the way of Cincinnati, and down the Ohio and Mississippi. My idea was to take ship, at New Orleans, for Para. In New Orleans I inquired, and found there was no ship leaving for Para. Also, that there had never *been* one leaving for Para. I reflected. A policeman came and asked me what I was doing, and I told him. He made me move on; and said if he caught me reflecting in the public street again he would run me in.

After a few days I was out of money. Then Circumstance arrived, with another turning point in my life—a new link. On my way down, I had made the acquaintance of a pilot; I begged him to teach me the river, and he consented. I became a pilot.

By and by Circumstance came again—introducing the Civil War, this time, in order to push me ahead a stage or two toward the literary profession. The boats stopped running, my livelihood was gone.

Circumstance came to the rescue with a new turning point and a fresh link. My brother was appointed secretary to the new Territory of Nevada, and he invited me to go with him and help him in his office. I accepted.

In Nevada, Circumstance furnished me the silver fever and I went into the mines to make a fortune and enter the ministry. As I supposed; but that was not the idea. The idea was, to move me another step toward literature. For amusement I scribbled things for the Virginia City *Enterprise*. One isn't a printer ten years without setting up acres of good and bad literature, and learning—unconsciously at first, consciously later—to discriminate between the two, within his mental limitations; and meantime he is unconsciously acquiring what is called a "style." One of my efforts attracted attention, and the *Enterprise* sent for me, and put me on its staff.

And so I became a journalist—another link. By and by Circumstance and the Sacramento *Union* sent me to the Sandwich Islands for five or six months, to write up sugar. I did it; and threw in a good deal of extraneous matter that hadn't anything to do with sugar. But it was extraneous matter that helped me to another link.

It made me notorious, and San Francisco invited me to lecture. Which I did. And profitably. I had long had a desire to travel and see the world, and now the platform had furnished me the means. So I joined the "Quaker City Excursion."

When I returned to America, Circumstance was waiting on the pier—with the *last* link: I was asked to *write a book*, and I did it, and called it *The Innocents Abroad*. Thus at last I became a member of the literary guild. That was forty-two years ago, and I have been a member ever since. Leaving the Rubicon incident away back where it belongs, I can say with truth that the reason I am in the literary profession is because I had the measles when I was twelve years old.

III

Now what interests me, as regards these details, is not the details themselves, but the fact that none of them was foreseen by me, none of them was planned by me, I was the author of none of them. Circumstance, working in harness with my temperament, created them all and compelled them all. I often offered help, and with the best intentions, but it was rejected: as a rule, uncourteously. I could never plan a thing and get it to come out the way I planned it. It came out some other way—some way I had not counted upon.

And so I do not admire the human being—as an intellectual marvel—as much as I did when I was young, and got him out of books, and did not know him personally. When I used to read that such and such a general did a certain brilliant thing, I believed it. Whereas it was not so. Circumstance did it, by help of his temperament. The circumstances would have failed of effect with a general of another temperament: he might see the chance, but lose the advantage by being by nature too slow or too quick or too doubtful. Once General Grant was asked a question about a matter which had been much debated by the public and the newspapers; he answered the question without any hesitancy: "General, who planned the march through Georgia?" "The enemy!" He added that the enemy usually makes your plans for you. He meant that the enemy, by neglect or through force of circumstances, leaves an opening for you, and you see your chance and take advantage of it.

Circumstances do the planning for us all, no doubt, by help of our temperaments. I see no great difference between a man and a watch, except that the man is conscious and the watch isn't, and the man *tries* to plan things and the watch doesn't. The watch doesn't wind itself, and doesn't regulate itself—these things are done exteriorly. Outside influences, outside circumstances, wind the *man* and regulate him. Left to himself he wouldn't get regulated at all, and the sort of time he would keep would not be valuable. Some rare men are wonderful watches, with gold case, compensation balance, and all those things, and some men are only sweet and humble Waterburys. I am a Waterbury. A Waterbury of that kind, some say.

A nation is only an individual, multiplied. It makes plans, and Circumstance comes and upsets them—or enlarges them. A gang of patriots throws the tea overboard; it destroys a Bastile. The plans stop there; then Circumstance comes in, quite unexpectedly, and turns those modest riots into a revolution.

And there was poor Columbus. He elaborated a deep plan to find a new route to an old country. Circumstance revised his plan for him, and he found a new *world*. And *he* gets the credit of it, to this day. He hadn't anything to do with it.

Necessarily the scene of the real turning point in my life (and of yours) was the Garden of Eden. It was there that the first link was forged of the chain that was ultimately to lead to the emptying of me into the literary guild. Adam's *temperament* was the first command the Deity ever issued to a human being on this planet. And it was the only command Adam would *never* be able to disobey. It said, "Be weak, be water, be characterless, be cheaply persuadable." The later command, to let the fruit alone, was certain to be disobeyed. Not by Adam himself, but by his *temperament*—which he did not create and had no authority over. For the *temperament* is the man; the thing tricked out with clothes and named Man, is merely its Shadow, nothing more. The law of the tiger's temperament is, Thou shalt kill; the law of the sheep's temperament is, Thou shalt not kill. To issue later commands requiring the tiger to let the fat stranger alone, and requiring the sheep to imbue its hands in the blood of the lion is not worth while, for those commands *can't* be obeyed. They would invite to violations of the law of *temperament*, which is supreme, and takes precedence over all other authorities. I cannot help feeling disappointed in Adam and Eve. That is, in their temperaments. Not in *them*, poor helpless young creatures—afflicted with temperaments made out of butter; which butter was commanded to get into contact with fire and *be melted*. What I cannot help wishing is, that Adam and Eve had been postponed, and Martin Luther and Joan of Arc put in their place—that splendid pair equipped with temperaments made not of butter, but of asbestos. By neither sugary persuasions nor hellfire could Satan have beguiled *them* to eat the apple.

There would have been results! Indeed yes. The apple would be intact to-day: there would be no human race; there would be no *you*, there would be no *me*. And the old, old creation-dawn scheme of ultimately launching me into the literary guild would have been defeated.

IV.

AMERICA AND AMERICANS

PLYMOUTH ROCK AND THE PILGRIMS

What do you want to celebrate those people for?—those ancestors of yours of 1620—the *Mayflower* tribe, I mean. What do you want to celebrate *them* for? Your pardon: the gentleman at my left assures me that you are not celebrating the Pilgrims themselves, but the landing of the Pilgrims at Plymouth Rock on the 22d of December. So you are celebrating their landing. Why, the other pretext was thin enough, but this is thinner than ever; the other was tissue, tinfoil, fish-bladder, but this is gold-leaf. Celebrating their landing! What was there remarkable about it, I would like to know? What can you be thinking of? Why, those Pilgrims had been at sea three or four months. It was the very middle of winter: it was cold as death off Cape Cod there. Why shouldn't they come ashore? If they *hadn't* landed there would be some reason for celebrating the fact. It would have been a case of monumental leatherheadedness which the world would not willingly let die. If it had been *you*, gentlemen, you probably wouldn't have landed, but you have no shadow of right to be celebrating, in your ancestors, gifts which they did not exercise, but only transmitted. Why, to be celebrating the mere landing of the Pilgrims—to be trying to make out that this most natural and simple and customary procedure was an extraordinary circumstance—a circumstance to be amazed at, and admired, aggrandized and glorified, at orgies like this for two hundred and sixty years—hang it, a horse would have known enough to land;

a horse— Pardon again; the gentleman on my right assures me that it was not merely the landing of the Pilgrims that we are celebrating, but the Pilgrims themselves. So we have struck an inconsistency here—one says it was the landing, the other says it was the Pilgrims. It is an inconsistency characteristic of your intractable and disputatious tribe, for you never agree about anything but Boston. Well, then, what do you want to celebrate those Pilgrims for? They were a mighty hard lot—you know it. I grant you, without the slightest unwillingness, that they were a great deal more gentle and merciful and just than were the people of Europe of that day; I grant you that they are better than their predecessors. But what of that?—that is nothing. People always progress. You are better than your fathers and grandfathers were (this is the first time I have ever aimed a measureless slander at the departed, for I consider such things improper). Yes, those among you who have not been in the penitentiary, if such there be, are better than your fathers and your grandfathers were; but is that any sufficient reason for getting up annual dinners and celebrating you? No, by no means—by no means. Well, I repeat, those Pilgrims were a hard lot. They took good care of themselves, but they abolished everybody else's ancestors. I am a border-ruffian from the State of Missouri. I am a Connecticut Yankee by adoption. In me, you have Missouri morals, Connecticut culture; this, gentleman, is the combination which makes the perfect man. But where are my ancestors? Whom shall I celebrate? Where shall I find the raw material?

My first American ancestor, gentlemen, was an Indian— an early Indian. Your ancestors skinned him alive, and I am an orphan. Not one drop of my blood flows in that Indian's veins to-day. I stand here, lone and forlorn, without an ancestor. They skinned him! I do not object to that, if they needed his fur; but alive, gentlemen—alive! They skinned him alive—and before company! That is what rankles. Think how he must have felt; for he was a sensitive person and easily embarrassed. If he had been a bird, it would have been all right, and no violence done to his feelings, because he would have been considered "dressed." But he was not a bird, gentlemen, he was a man, and probably one of the most undressed men that ever was. I ask you to put yourselves in his place. I ask it as a favor; I ask it as a tardy act of justice; I ask it in the interest of fidelity to the traditions of your ancestors; I ask it that the world may contemplate, with vision unobstructed by disguising swallow-tails and white cravats, the spectacle which the true New England Society ought to present. Cease to come to these annual orgies in this hollow modern mockery—the surplusage of raiment. Come in character; come in the summer grace, come in the unadorned simplicity, come in the free and joyous costume which your sainted ancestors provided for mine.

Later ancestors of mine were the Quakers William Robinson, Marmaduke Stevenson, *et al.* Your tribe chased them out of the country for their religion's sake; promised them death if they came back; for your ancestors had forsaken the homes they loved, and braved the perils of the sea, the implacable climate, and the savage wilderness, to acquire that highest and most precious of boons, freedom for every man on this broad continent to worship according to the dictates of his own conscience—and they were not going to allow a lot of pestiferous Quakers to interfere with it. Your ancestors broke forever the chains of political slavery, and gave the vote to every man in this wide land, excluding none!—none except those who did not belong to the orthodox church. Your ancestors—yes, they were a hard lot; but, nevertheless, they gave us religious liberty to worship as they required us to worship, and political liberty to vote as the church required; and so I the bereft one, I the forlorn one, am here to do my best to help you celebrate them right.

The Quaker woman Elizabeth Hooton was an ancestress of mine. Your people were pretty severe with her—you will confess that. But, poor thing! I believe they changed her opinions before she died, and took her into their fold; and so we have every reason to presume that when she died she went to the same place which your ancestors went to. It is a great pity, for she was a good woman. Roger Williams was an ancestor of mine. I don't really remember what your people did with him. But they banished him to Rhode Island, anyway. And then, I believe, recognizing that this was really carrying harshness to an unjustifiable extreme, they took pity on him and burned him. They were a hard lot! All those Salem witches were ancestors of mine! Your people made it tropical for them. Yes, they did; by pressure and the gallows they made such a clean deal with them that there hasn't been a witch and hardly a halter in our family from that day to this, and that is one hundred and eighty-nine years. The first slave brought into New England out of Africa by your progenitors was an ancestor of mine—for I am of a mixed breed, an infinitely shaded and exquisite Mongrel. I'm not one of your sham meerschaums that you can color in a week. No, my complexion is the patient art of eight generations. Well, in my own time, I had acquired a lot of my kin—by purchase, and swapping around, and one way and another—and was getting along very well. Then, with the inborn perversity of your lineage, you got up a war, and took them all away from me. And so, again am I bereft, again am I forlorn; no drop of my blood flows in the veins of any living being who is marketable.

O my friends, hear me and reform! I seek your good, not mine. You have heard the speeches. Disband these New

England societies—nurseries of a system of steadily augmenting laudation and hosannaing, which, if persisted in uncurbed, may some day in the remote future beguile you into prevaricating and bragging. Oh, stop, stop, while you are still temperate in your appreciation of your ancestors! Hear me, I beseech you; get up an auction and sell Plymouth Rock! The Pilgrims were a simple and ignorant race. They never had seen any good rocks before, or at least any that were not watched, and so they were excusable for hopping ashore in frantic delight and clapping an iron fence around this one. But you, gentlemen, are educated; you are enlightened; you know that in the rich land of your nativity, opulent New England, overflowing with rocks, this one isn't worth, at the outside, more than thirty-five cents. Therefore, sell it, before it is injured by exposure, or at least throw it open to the patent-medicine advertisements, and let it earn its taxes.

Yes, hear your true friend—your only true friend—list to his voice. Disband these societies, hotbeds of vice, of moral decay—perpetuators of ancestral superstition. Here on this board I see water, I see milk, I see the wild and deadly lemonade. These are but the steps upon the downward path. Next we shall see tea, then chocolate, then coffee—hotel coffee. A few more years—all too few, I fear—mark my words, we shall have cider! Gentlemen, pause ere it be too late. You are on the broad road which leads to dissipation, physical ruin, moral decay, gory crime and the gallows! I beseech you, I implore you, in the name of your anxious friends, in the name of your suffering families, in the name of your impending widows and orphans, stop ere it be too late. Disband these New England societies, renounce these soul-blistering saturnalia, cease from varnishing the rusty reputations of your long-vanished ancestors—the super-high-moral old iron-clads of Cape Cod, the pious buccaneers of Plymouth Rock—go home, and try to learn to behave!

However, chaff and nonsense aside, I think I honor and appreciate your Pilgrim stock as much as you do yourselves, perhaps; and I endorse and adopt a sentiment uttered by a grandfather of mine once—a man of sturdy opinions, of sincere make of mind, and not given to flattery. He said: "People may talk as they like about that Pilgrim stock, but, after all's said and done, it would be pretty hard to improve on those people; and, as for me, I don't mind coming out flatfooted and saying there ain't any way to improve on them—except having them born in Missouri!"

The Weather

I reverently believe that the Maker who made us all makes everything in New England but the weather. I don't know who makes that, but I think it must be raw apprentices in the weather-clerk's factory who experiment and learn how, in New England, for board and clothes, and then are promoted to make weather for countries that require a good article, and will take their custom elsewhere if they don't get it. There is a sumptuous variety about the New England weather that compels the stranger's admiration—and regret. The weather is always doing something there; always attending strictly to business; always getting up new designs and trying them on the people to see how they will go. But it gets through more business in spring than in any other season. In the spring I have counted one hundred and thirty-six different kinds of weather inside of four-and-twenty hours. It was I that made the fame and fortune of that man that had that marvellous collection of weather on exhibition at the Centennial, that so astounded the foreigners. He was going to travel all over the world and get specimens from all the climes. I said, "Don't you do it; you come to New England on a favorable spring day." I told him what we could do in the way of style, variety, and quantity. Well, he came and he made his collection in four days. As to variety, why, he confessed that he got hundreds of kinds of weather that he had never heard of before. And as to quantity—well, after he had picked out and discarded all that was blemished in any way, he not only had weather enough, but weather to spare; weather to hire out; weather to sell; to deposit; weather to invest; weather to give to the poor. The people of New England are by nature patient and forbearing, but there are some things which they will not stand. Every year they kill a lot of poets for writing about "Beautiful Spring." These are generally casual visitors, who bring their notions of spring from somewhere else, and cannot, of course, know how the natives feel about spring. And so the first thing they know the opportunity to inquire how they feel has permanently gone by. Old Probabilities has a mighty reputation for accurate prophecy, and thoroughly well deserves it. You take up the paper and observe how crisply and confidently he checks off what to-day's weather is going to be on the Pacific, down South, in the Middle States, in the Wisconsin region. See him sail along in the joy and pride of his power till he gets to New England, and then see his tail drop. *He* doesn't know what the weather is going to be in New England. Well, he mulls over it, and by-and-by he gets out something about like this: Probably northeast to southwest winds, varying to the southward and westward and eastward, and points between, high and low barometer swapping around from place to place; probable areas of rain, snow, hail, and drought, succeeded or preceded by earthquakes, with thunder and lightning. Then he jots down his postscript from his wandering mind, to cover accidents. "But it is possible that the programme may be wholly changed in the mean time." Yes, one of the brightest gems in the New England weather is the dazzling uncertainty of it. There is only one thing certain about it: you are certain there is going to be plenty of it—a perfect grand review; but you never can tell which end of the procession is going to move first. You fix up for the drought; you leave your umbrella in the house and sally out, and two to one you get drowned. You make up your mind that the earthquake is due; you stand from under, and take hold of something to steady yourself, and the first thing you know you get struck by lightning. These are great disappointments; but they can't be helped. The lightning there is peculiar; it is so convincing, that when it strikes a thing it doesn't leave enough of that thing behind for you to tell whether— Well, you'd think it was something valuable, and a Congressman had been there. And the thunder. When the thunder begins to merely tune up and scrape and saw, and key up the instruments for the performance, strangers say, "Why, what awful thunder you have here!" But when the baton is raised and the real concert begins, you'll find that stranger down in the cellar with his head in the ash-barrel. Now as to the *size* of the weather in New England—lengthways, I mean. It is utterly disproportioned to the size of that little country. Half the time, when it is packed as full as it can stick, you will see that New England weather sticking out beyond the edges and projecting around hundreds and hundreds of miles over the neighboring States. She can't hold a tenth part of her weather. You can see cracks all about where she has strained herself trying to do it. I could speak volumes about the inhuman perversity of the New England weather, but I will give but a single specimen. I like to hear rain on a tin roof. So I covered part of my roof with tin, with an eye to that luxury. Well, sir, do you think it ever rains on that tin? No, sir; skips it every time. Mind, in this speech I have been trying merely to do honor to the New England weather—no language could do it justice. But, after all, there is at least one or two things about that weather (or, if you please, effects produced by it) which we residents would not like to part with. If we hadn't our bewitching autumn foliage, we should have to credit the weather with one feature which compensates for all its bullying vagaries—the ice-storm: when a leafless tree is clothed with ice from the bottom to the top—ice that is as bright and clear as crystal; when every bough and twig is strung with ice-beads, frozen dew-drops, and the whole tree sparkles cold and white, like the Shah of Persia's diamond plume. Then the wind waves the branches and the sun comes out and turns all those myriads of beads and drops to prisms that glow and burn and flash with all manner of colored fires, which change and change again with inconceivable rapidity from blue to red, from red to green, and green to gold—the tree becomes a spraying fountain, a very explosion of dazzling jewels; and it stands there the acme, the climax, the supremest possibility in art or nature, of bewildering, intoxicating, intolerable magnificence. One cannot make the words too strong.

New York City*

In this absence of nine years I find a great improvement in the city of New York. I am glad to speak on that as a toast—"The City of New York." Some say it has improved because I have been away. Others, and I agree with them, say it has improved because I have come back. We must judge of a city, as of a man, by its external appearances and by its inward character. In externals the foreigner coming to these shores is more impressed at first by our sky-scrapers. They are new to him. He has not done anything of the sort since he built the tower of Babel. The foreigner is shocked by them.

In the daylight they are ugly. They are—well, too chimneyfied and too snaggy—like a mouth that needs attention from a dentist; like a cemetery that is all monuments and no gravestones. But at night, seen from the river where they are columns towering against the sky, all sparkling with light, they are fairylike; they are beauty more satisfactory to the soul and more enchanting than anything that man has dreamed of since the Arabian nights. We can't always have the beautiful aspect of things. Let us make the most of our sights that are beautiful and let the others go. When your foreigner makes disagreeable comments on New York by daylight, float him down the river at night.

What has made these sky-scrapers possible is the eleva-

*Editor's title.

tor. The cigar-box which the European calls a "lift" needs but to be compared with our elevators to be appreciated. The lift stops to reflect between floors. That is all right in a hearse, but not in elevators. The American elevator acts like the man's patent purge—it worked. As the inventor said, "This purge doesn't waste any time fooling around; it attends strictly to business."

That New-Yorkers have the cleanest, quickest, and most admirable system of street railways in the world has been forced upon you by the abnormal appreciation you have of your hackman. We ought always to be grateful to him for that service. Nobody else would have brought such a system into existence for us. We ought to build him a monument. We owe him one as much as we owe one to anybody. Let is be a tall one. Nothing permanent, of course; build it of plaster, say. Then gaze at it and realize how grateful we are—for the time being—and then pull it down and throw it on the ash-heap. That's the way to honor your public heroes.

As to our streets, I find them cleaner than they used to be. I miss those dear old landmarks, the symmetrical mountain ranges of dust and dirt that used to be piled up along the streets for the wind and rain to tear down at their pleasure. Yes, New York is cleaner than Bombay. I realize that I have been in Bombay, that I am now in New York; that it is not my duty to flatter Bombay, but rather to flatter New York.

Compared with the wretched attempts of London to light that city, New York may fairly be said to be a well-lighted city. Why, London's attempt at good lighting is almost as bad as London's attempt at rapid transit. There is just one good system of rapid transit in London—the "Tube," and that, of course, had been put in by Americans. Perhaps, after a while, those Americans will come back and give New York also a good underground system. Perhaps they have already begun. I have been so busy since I came back that I haven't had time as yet to go down cellar.

But it is by the laws of the city, it is by the manners of the city, it is by the ideals of the city, it is by the customs of the city and by the municipal government which all these elements correct, support, and foster, by which the foreigner judges the city. It is by these that he realizes that New York may, indeed, hold her head high among the cities of the world. It is by these standards that he knows whether to class the city higher or lower than the other municipalities of the world.

Gentlemen, you have the best municipal government in the world—the purest and the most fragrant. The very angels envy you, and wish they could establish a government like it in heaven. You got it by a noble fidelity to civic duty. You got it by stern and ever-watchful exertion of the great powers with which you are charged by the rights which were handed down to you by your forefathers, by your manly refusal to let base men invade the high places of your government, and by instant retaliation when any public officer has insulted you in the city's name by swerving in the slightest from the upright and full performance of his duty. It is you who have made this city the envy of the cities of the world. God will bless you for it—God will bless you for it. Why, when you approach the final resting-place the angels of heaven will gather at the gates and cry out:

"Here they come! Show them to the archangel's box, and turn the lime-light on them!"

Taxes and Morals

Every born American among the eighty millions, let his creed or destitution of creed be what it may, is indisputably a Christian to this degree—that his moral constitution is Christian.

There are two kinds of Christian morals, one private and the other public. These two are so distinct, so unrelated, that they are no more akin to each other than are archangels and politicians. During three-hundred and sixty-three days in the year the American citizen is true to his Christian private morals, and keeps undefiled the nation's character at its best and highest; then in the other two days of the year he leaves his Christian private morals at home and carries his Christian public morals to the tax office and the polls, and does the best he can to damage and undo his whole year's faithful and righteous work. Without a blush he will vote for an unclean boss if that boss is his party's Moses, without compunction he will vote against the best man in the whole land if he is on the other ticket. Every year in a number of cities and States he helps put corrupt men in office, whereas if he would but throw away his Christian public morals, and carry his Christian private morals to the polls, he could promptly purify the public service and make the possession of office a high and honorable distinction.

Once a year he lays aside his Christian private morals and hires a ferry-boat and piles up his bonds in a warehouse in New Jersey for three days, and gets out his Christian public morals and goes to the tax office and holds up his hands and swears he wishes he may never-never if he's got a cent in the world, so help him. The next day the list appears in the papers—a column and a quarter of names, in fine print, and every man in the list a billionaire and member of a couple of churches. I know all those people. I have friendly, social, and criminal relations with the whole lot of them. They never miss a sermon when they are so's to be around, and they never miss swearing-off day, whether they are so's be around or not.

I used to be an honest man. I am crumbling. No—I have crumbled. When they assessed me at $75,000 a fortnight ago I went out and tried to borrow the money, and couldn't; then when I found they were letting a whole crop of millionaires live in New York at a third of the price they were charging me I was hurt, I was indignant, and said: "This is the last feather. I am not going to run this town all by myself." In that moment—in that memorable moment—I began to crumble. In fifteen minutes the disintegration was complete. In fifteen minutes I had become just a mere moral sand-pile; and I lifted up my hand along with those seasoned and experienced deacons and swore off every rag of personal property I've got in the world, clear down to cork leg, glass eye, and what is left of my wig.

Those tax officers were moved; they were profoundly moved. They had long been accustomed to seeing hardened old grafters act like that, and they could endure the spectacle; but they were expecting better things of me, a chartered, professional moralist, and they were saddened.

I fell visibly in their respect and esteem, and I should have fallen in my own, except that I had already struck bottom, and there wasn't any place to fall to.

Characteristics of Americans*

There isn't a single human characteristic that can be safely labeled American. There isn't a single human ambition, or religious trend, or drift of thought, or peculiarity of education, or code of principles, or breed of folly, or style of conversation, or preference for a particular subject for discussion, or form of legs or trunk or head or face or expression or complexion, or gait, or dress, or manners, or disposition, or any other human detail, inside or outside, that can rationally be generalized as American.

Whenever you have found what seems to be an American peculiarity, you have only to cross a frontier or two, or go down or up in the social scale, and you perceive that it has disappeared. And you can cross the Atlantic and find it again. There may be a Newport religious drift or sporting drift, or conversational style or complexion, or cut of face, but there are entire empires in America, north, south, east, and west, where you could not find your duplicates. It is the same with everything else which one might propose to call American. M. Bourget thinks he has found the American Coquette. If he had really found her he would also have found, I am sure, that she was not new, that she exists in other lands in the same forms, and with the same frivolous heart and the same ways and impulses. I think this because I have seen our coquette; I have seen her in life; better

*Editor's title.

still, I have seen her in our novels, and seen her twin in foreign novels. I wish M. Bourget had seen ours. He thought he saw her. And so he applied his System to her. She was a Species. So he gathered a number of samples of what seemed to be her, and put them under his glass, and divided them into groups which he calls types, and labelled them in his usual scientific way with "formulas"—brief, sharp descriptive flashes that make a person blink, sometimes, they are so sudden and vivid. As a rule they are pretty far-fetched, but that is not an important matter; they surprise, they compel admiration, and I notice by some of the comments which his efforts have called forth that they deceive the unwary. Here are a few of the coquette variants which he has grouped and labeled:

> THE COLLECTOR.
> THE EQUILIBREE.
> THE PROFESSIONAL BEAUTY.
> THE BLUFFER.
> THE GIRL-BOY.

If he had stopped with describing these characters we should have been obliged to believe that they exist; that they exist, and that he has seen them and spoken with them. But he did not stop there; he went further and furnished to us light-throwing samples of their behavior, and also light-throwing samples of their speeches. He entered those things in his note-book without suspicion, he takes them out and delivers them to the world with a candor and simplicity which show that he believed them genuine. They throw altogether too much light. They reveal to the native the origin of his find. I suppose he knows how he came to make that novel and captivating discovery, by this time. If he does not, any American can tell him—any American to whom he will show his anecdotes. It was "put up" on him, as we say. It was a jest—to be plain, it was a series of frauds. To my mind it was a poor sort of jest, witless and contemptible. The players of it have their reward, such as it is; they have exhibited the fact that whatever they may be they are not ladies. M. Bourget did not discover a type of coquette; he merely discovered a type of practical joker. One may say *the* type of practical joker, for these people are exactly alike all over the world. Their equipment is always the same: a vulgar mind, a puerile wit, a cruel disposition as a rule, and always the spirit of treachery.

In his Chapter IV. M. Bourget has two or three columns gravely devoted to the collating and examining and psychologizing of these sorry little frauds. One is not moved to laugh. There is nothing funny in the situation; it is only pathetic. The stranger gave those people his confidence, and they dishonorably treated him in return.

But one must be allowed to suspect that M. Bourget was a little to blame himself. Even a practical joker has some little judgment. He has to exercise some degree of sagacity in selecting his prey if he would save himself from getting into trouble. In my time I have seldom seen such daring things marketed at any price as these conscienceless folk have worked off at par on this confiding observer. It compels the conviction that there was something about him that bred in those speculators a quite unusual sense of safety, and encouraged them to strain their powers in his behalf. They seem to have satisfied themselves that all he wanted was significant facts, and that he was not accustomed to examine the source whence they proceeded. It is plain that there was a sort of conspiracy against him almost from the start—a conspiracy to freight him up with all the strange extravagances those people's decayed brains could invent.

The lengths to which they went are next to incredible. They told him things which surely would have excited any one else's suspicion, but they did not excite his. Consider this:

> "There is not in all the United States an entirely nude statue."

If an angel should come down and say such a thing about heaven, a reasonably cautious observer would take that angel's number and inquire a little further before he added it to his catch. What does the present observer do? Adds it. Adds it at once. Adds it, and labels it with this innocent comment:

> "This smallest fact is strangely significant."

It does seem to me that this kind of observing is defective.

Here is another curiosity which some liberal person made him a present of. I should think it ought to have disturbed the deep slumber of his suspicion a little, but it didn't. It was a note from a fog-horn for strenuousness, it seems to me, but the doomed voyager did not catch it. If he had but caught it, it would have saved him from several disasters:

> "If the American knows that you are travelling to take notes, he is interested in it, and at the same time rejoices in it, as in a tribute."

Again, this is defective observation. It is human to like to be praised; one can even notice it in the French. But it is not human to like to be ridiculed, even when it comes in the form of a "tribute." I think a little psychologizing ought to have come in there. Something like this: A dog does not like to be ridiculed, a redskin does not like to be ridiculed, a negro does not like to be ridiculed, a Chinaman does not like to be ridiculed; let us deduce from these significant facts this formula: the American's grade being higher than these, and the chain of argument stretching unbroken all the way up to him, there is room for suspicion that the person who said the American likes to be ridiculed, and regards it as a tribute, is not a capable observer.

I feel persuaded that in the matter of psychologizing, a professional is too apt to yield to the fascinations of the loftier regions of that great art, to the neglect of its lowlier walks. Every now and then, at half-hour intervals, M. Bourget collects a hatful of airy inaccuracies and dissolves them in a panful of assorted abstractions, and runs the charge into a mould and turns you out a compact principle which will explain an American girl, or an American woman, or why new people yearn for old things, or any other impossible riddle which a person wants answered.

It seems to be conceded that there are a few human peculiarities that can be generalized and located here and there in the world and named by the name of the nation where they are found. I wonder what they are. Perhaps one of them is temperament. One speaks of French vivacity and German gravity and English stubbornness. There is no American temperament. The nearest that one can come at it is to say there are two—the composed Northern and the impetuous Southern; and both are found in other countries. Morals? Purity of women may fairly be called universal with us, but that is the case in some other countries. We have no monopoly of it; it cannot be named American. I think that there is but a single specialty with us, only one thing that can be called by the wide name American. That is the national devotion to ice-water. All Germans drink beer, but the British nation drinks beer, too; so neither of those peoples is the beer-drinking nation. I suppose we do stand alone in having a drink that nobody likes but ourselves. When we have been a month in Europe we lose our craving for it, and we finally tell the hotel folk that they needn't provide it any more. Yet we hardly touch our native shore again, winter or summer, before we are eager for it. The reasons for this state of things have not been psychologized yet. I drop the hint and say no more.

It is my belief that there are some "national" traits and things scattered about the world that are mere superstitions, frauds that have lived so long that they have the solid look of facts. One of them is the dogma that the French are the only chaste people in the world. Ever since I arrived in France this last time I have been accumulating doubts about that; and before I leave this sunny land again I will gather in a few random statistics and psychologize the plausibilities out of it. If people are to come over to America and find fault with our girls and our women, and psychologize every little thing they do, and try to teach them how to behave, and how to cultivate themselves up to where one cannot tell them from the French model, I intend to find out whether those missionaries are qualified or not. A nation ought always to examine into this detail before engaging the teacher for good. This last one has let fall a remark which renewed those doubts of mine when I read it:

"In our high Parisian existence, for instance, we find applied to arts and luxury, and to debauchery, all the powers and all the weaknesses of the French soul."

You see, it amounts to a trade with the French soul; a profession; a science; the serious business of life, so to speak, in our high Parisian existence. I do not quite like the look of it. I question if it can be taught with profit in our country, except of course to those pathetic, neglected minds that are waiting there so yearningly for the education which M.

Bourget is going to furnish them from the serene summits of our high Parisian life.

I spoke a moment ago of the existence of some superstitions that have been parading the world as facts this long time. For instance, consider the Dollar. The world seems to think that the love of money is "American"; and that the mad desire to get suddenly rich is "American." I believe that both of these things are merely and broadly human, not American monopolies at all. The love of money is natural to all nations, for money is a good and strong friend. I think that this love has existed everywhere, ever since the Bible called it the root of all evil.

I think that the reason why we Americans seem to be so addicted to trying to get rich suddenly is merely because the *opportunity* to make promising efforts in that direction has offered itself to us with a frequency out of all proportion to the European experience. For eighty years this opportunity has been offering itself in one new town or region after another straight westward, step by step, all the way from the Atlantic coast to the Pacific. When a mechanic could buy ten town lots on tolerably long credit for ten months' savings out of his wages, and reasonably expect to sell them in a couple of years for ten times what he gave for them, it was human for him to try the venture, and he did it no matter what his nationality was. He would have done it in Europe or China if he had had the same chance.

In the flush times in the silver regions a cook or any other humble worker stood a very good chance to get rich out of a trifle of money risked in a stock deal; and that person promptly took that risk, no matter what his or her nationality might be. I was there, and saw it.

But these opportunities have not been plenty in our Southern States; so there you have a prodigious region where the rush for sudden wealth is almost an unknown thing—and has been, from the beginning. Europe has offered few opportunities for poor Tom, Dick, and Harry; but when she has offered one, there has been no noticeable difference between European eagerness and American. England saw this in the wild days of the Railroad King; France saw it in 1720—time of Law and the Mississippi Bubble. I am sure I have never seen in the gold and silver mines any madness, fury, frenzy to get suddenly rich which was even remotely comparable to that which raged in France in the Bubble day. If I had a cyclopaedia here I could turn to that memorable case, and satisfy nearly anybody that the hunger for the sudden dollar is no more "American" than it is French. And if I could furnish an American opportunity to staid Germany, I think I could wake her up like a house afire.

But I must return to the Generalizations, Psychologizings, Deductions. When M. Bourget is exploiting these arts, it is then that he is peculiarly and particularly himself. His ways are wholly original when he encounters a trait or a custom which is new to him. Another person would merely examine the find, verify it, estimate its value, and let it go; but that is not sufficient for M. Bourget: he always wants to know *why* that thing exists, he wants to know how it came to happen; and he will not let go of it until he has found out. And in every instance he will find that reason where no one but himself would have thought of looking for it. He does not seem to care for a reason that is not picturesquely located; one might almost say picturesquely and impossibly located.

He found out that in America men do not try to hunt down young married women. At once, as usual, he wanted to know *why*. Any one could have told him. He could have divined it by the lights thrown by the novels of the country.

But no, he preferred to find out for himself. He has a trustfulness as regards men and facts which is fine and unusual; he is not particular about the source of a fact, he is not particular about the character and standing of the fact itself; but when it comes to pounding out the reason for the existence of the fact, he will trust no one but himself.

In the present instance here was his fact: American young married women are not pursued by the corruptor; and here was the question: What is it that protects her?

It seems quite unlikely that that problem could have offered difficulties to any but a trained philosopher. Nearly any person would have said to M. Bourget: "Oh, that is very simple. It is very seldom in America that a marriage is made on a commercial basis; our marriages, from the beginning, have been made for love; and where love is there is no room for the corruptor."

Now, it is interesting to see the formidable way in which M. Bourget went at that poor, humble little thing. He moved upon it in column—three columns—and with artillery.

"Two reasons of a very different kind explain"—that fact.

And now that I have got so far, I am almost afraid to say what his two reasons are, lest I be charged with inventing them. But I will not retreat now; I will condense them and print them, giving my word that I am honest, and not trying to deceive any one.

1. Young married women are protected from the approaches of the seducer in New England and vicinity by the diluted remains of a prudence created by a Puritan law of two hundred years ago, which for a while punished adultery with death.
2. And young married women of the other forty or fifty States are protected by laws which afford extraordinary facilities for divorce.

If I have not lost my mind I have accurately conveyed those two Vesuvian irruptions of philosophy. But the reader can consult Chapter IV. of *Outre-Mer* and decide for himself. Let us examine this paralyzing Deduction or Explanation by the light of a few sane facts.

1. This universality of protection has existed in our country *from the beginning;* before the death penalty existed in New England, and during all the generations that have dragged by since it was annulled.
2. Extraordinary facilities for divorce are of such recent creation that any middle-aged American can remember a time when such things had not yet been thought of.

Let us suppose that the first easy divorce law went into effect forty years ago, and got noised around and fairly started in business thirty-five years ago, when we had, say, 25,000,000 of white population. Let us suppose that among 5,000,000 of them the young married women were protected by the surviving shudder of that ancient Puritan scare—what is M. Bourget going to do about those who lived among the 20,000,000? They were clean in their morals, they were pure, yet there was no easy divorce law to protect them.

Awhile ago I said that M. Bourget's method of truth-seeking—hunting for it in out-of-the-way places—was new; but that was an error. I remember that when Leverrier discovered the Milky Way, he and the other astronomers began to theorize about it in substantially the same fashion which M. Bourget employs in his reasonings about American social facts and their origin. Leverrier advanced the hypothesis that the Milky Way was caused by gaseous protoplasmic emanations from the field of Waterloo, which, ascending to an altitude determinable by their own specific gravity, became luminous through the development and exposure—by the natural processes of animal decay—of the phosphorus contained in them.

This theory was warmly complimented by Ptolemy, who, however, after much thought and research, decided that he could not accept it as final. His own theory was that the Milky Way was an emigration of lightning-bugs; and he supported and reinforced this theorem by the well-known fact that the locusts do like that in Egypt.

Giordano Bruno also was outspoken in his praises of Leverrier's important contribution to astronomical science, and was at first inclined to regard it as conclusive; but later, conceiving it to be erroneous, he pronounced against it, and advanced the hypothesis that the Milky Way was a detachment or corps of stars which became arrested and held in *suspenso suspensorum* by refraction of gravitation while on the march to join their several constellations; a proposition for which he was afterwards burned at the stake in Jacksonville, Illinois.

These were all brilliant and picturesque theories, and each was received with enthusiasm by the scientific world; but when a New England farmer, who was not a thinker, but only a plain sort of person who tried to account for large facts in simple ways, came out with the opinion that the Milky Way was just common, ordinary stars, and was put where it was because God "wanted to hev it so," the admirable idea fell perfectly flat.

As a literary artist, M. Bourget is as fresh and striking as he is as a scientific one. He says, "Above all, I do not believe much in anecdotes." Why? "In history they are all false"—a sufficiently broad statement—"in literature all libelous"— also a sufficiently sweeping statement, coming from a critic who notes that we are a people who are peculiarly extravagant in our language—"and when it is a matter of social life, almost all biased." It seems to amount to stultification, almost. He has built two or three breeds of American coquettes out of anecdotes—mainly "biased" ones, I suppose; and, as they occur "in literature," furnished by his pen, they must be "all libelous." Or did he mean not *in* literature or anecdotes *about* literature or literary people? I am not able to answer that. Perhaps the original would be clearer, but I have only the translation of this installment by me. I think the remark had an intention; also that this intention was booked for the trip; but that either in the hurry of the remark's departure it got left, or in the confusion of changing cars at the translator's frontier it got side-tracked.

"But on the other hand I believe in statistics; and those on divorces appear to me to be most conclusive." And he sets himself the task of explaining—in a couple of columns—the process by which Easy-Divorce conceived, invented, originated, developed, and perfected an empire-embracing condition of sexual purity in the States. *In 40 years.* No, he doesn't state the interval. With all his passion for statistics he forgot to ask how long it took to produce this gigantic miracle.

I have followed his pleasant but devious trail through those columns, but I was not able to get hold of his argument and find out what it was. I was not even able to find out where it left off. It seemed to gradually dissolve and flow off into other matters. I followed it with interest, for I was anxious to learn how easy-divorce eradicated adultery in America, but I was disappointed; I have no idea yet how it did it. I only know it didn't. But that is not valuable; I knew it before.

Well, humor is the great thing, the saving thing, after all. The minute it crops up, all our hardnesses yield, all our irritations and resentments flit away, and a sunny spirit takes their place. And so, when M. Bourget said that bright thing about our grandfathers, I broke all up. I remember exploding its American countermine once, under that grand hero, Napoleon. He was only First Consul then, and I was Consul-General—for the United States, of course; but we were very intimate, notwithstanding the difference in rank, for I waived that. One day something offered the opening, and he said:

"Well, General, I suppose life can never get entirely dull to an American, because whenever he can't strike up any other way to put in his time he can always get away with a few years trying to find out who his grandfather was!"

I fairly shouted, for I had never heard it sound better; and then I was back at him as quick as a flash:

"Right, your Excellency! But I reckon a Frenchman's got *his* little stand-by for a dull time, too; because when all other interests fail he can turn in and see if he can't find out who his father was!"

Well, you should have heard him just whoop, and cackle, and carry on! He reached up and hit me one on the shoulder, and says:

"Land, but it's good! It's im-mensely good! I'George, I never heard it said so good in my life before! Say it again."

So I said it again, and he said his again, and I said mine again, and then he did, and then I did, and then he did, and we kept on doing it, and doing it, and I never had such a good time, and he said the same. In my opinion there isn't anything that is as killing as one of those dear old ripe pensioners if you know how to snatch it out in a kind of a fresh sort of original way.

But I wish M. Bourget had read more of our novels before he came. It is the only way to thoroughly understand a people. When I found I was coming to Paris, I read *La Terre*.

Disgraceful Persecution of a Boy

In San Francisco, the other day, "A well-dressed boy, on his way to Sunday-school, was arrested and thrown into the city prison for stoning Chinamen."

What a commentary is this upon human justice! What sad prominence it gives to our human disposition to tyrannize over the weak! San Francisco has little right to take credit to herself for her treatment of this poor boy. What had the child's education been? How should he suppose it was wrong to stone a Chinaman? Before we side against him, along with outraged San Francisco, let us give him a chance—let us hear the testimony for the defense.

He was a "well-dressed" boy, and a Sunday-school scholar, and, therefore the chances are that his parents were intelligent, well-to-do people, with just enough natural villany in their compositions to make them yearn after the daily papers, and enjoy them; and so this boy had opportunities to learn all through the week how to do right, as well as on Sunday.

It was in this way that he found out that the great commonwealth of California imposes an unlawful mining-tax upon John the foreigner, and allows Patrick the foreigner to dig gold for nothing—probably because the degraded Mongol is at no expense for whisky, and the refined Celt cannot exist without it.

It was in this way that he found out that a respectable

number of the tax-gatherers—it would be unkind to say all of them—collect the tax twice, instead of once; and that, inasmuch as they do it solely to discourage Chinese immigration into the mines, it is a thing that is much applauded, and likewise regarded as being singularly facetious.

It was in this way that he found out that when a white man robs a sluice-box (by the term white man is meant Spaniards, Mexicans, Portuguese, Irish, Hondurans, Peruvians, Chileans, etc., etc.), they make him leave the camp; and when a Chinaman does that thing, they hang him.

It was in this way that he found out that in many districts of the vast Pacific coast, so strong is the wild, free love of justice in the hearts of the people, that whenever any secret and mysterious crime is committed, they say, "Let justice be done, though the heavens fall," and go straightway and swing a Chinaman.

It was in this way that he found out that by studying one half of each day's "local items," it would appear that the police of San Francisco were either asleep or dead, and by studying the other half it would seem that the reporters were gone mad with admiration of the energy, the virtue, the high effectiveness, and the dare-devil intrepidity of that very police—making exultant mention of how "the Argus-eyed officer So-and-so" captured a wretched knave of a Chinaman who was stealing chickens, and brought him gloriously to the city prison; and how "the gallant officer Such-and-such-a-one" quietly kept an eye on the movements of an "unsuspecting almond-eyed son of Confucius" (your reporter is nothing if not facetious), following him around with that far-off look of vacancy and unconsciousness always so finely affected by that inscrutable being, the forty-dollar policeman, during a waking interval, and captured him at last in the very act of placing his hands in a suspicious manner upon a paper of tacks, left by the owner in an exposed situation; and how one officer performed this prodigious thing, and another officer that, and another the other—and pretty much every one of these performances having for a dazzling central incident a Chinaman guilty of a shilling's worth of crime, an unfortunate, whose misdemeanor must be hurrahed into something enormous in order to keep the public from noticing how many really important rascals went uncaptured in the mean time, and how overrated those glorified policemen actually are.

It was in this way that the boy found out that the legislature, being aware that the Constitution has made America an asylum for the poor and the oppressed of all nations, and that, therefore, the poor and oppressed who fly to our shelter must not be charged a disabling admission fee, made a law that every Chinaman, upon landing, must be *vaccinated* upon the wharf, and pay to the state's appointed officer *ten dollars* for the service, when there are plenty of doctors in San Francisco who would be glad enough to do it for him for fifty cents.

It was in this way that the boy found out that a Chinaman had no rights that any man was bound to respect; that he had no sorrows that any man was bound to pity; that neither his life nor his liberty was worth the purchase of a penny when a white man needed a scapegoat; that nobody loved Chinamen, nobody befriended them, nobody spared them suffering when it was convenient to inflict it; everybody, individuals, communities, the majesty of the state itself, joined in hating, abusing, and persecuting these humble strangers.

And, therefore, what *could* have been more natural than for this sunny-hearted boy, tripping along to Sunday-school, with his mind teeming with freshly learned incentives to high and virtuous action, to say to himself:

"Ah, there goes a Chinaman! God will not love me if I do not stone him."

And for this he was arrested and put in the city jail.

Everything conspired to teach him that it was a high and holy thing to stone a Chinaman, and yet he no sooner attempts to do his duty than he is punished for it—he, poor chap, who has been aware all his life that one of the principal recreations of the police, out toward the Gold Refinery, is to look on with tranquil enjoyment while the butchers of Brannan Street set their dogs on unoffending Chinamen, and make them flee for their lives.*

Keeping in mind the tuition in the humanities which the entire "Pacific coast" gives its youth, there is a very sublimity of grotesqueness in the virtuous flourish with which the good city fathers of San Francisco proclaim (as they have lately done) that "The police are positively ordered to arrest all boys, of every description and wherever found, who engage in assaulting Chinamen."

Still, let us be truly glad they have made the order, notwithstanding its prominent inconsistency; and let us rest perfectly confident the police are glad, too. Because there is no personal peril in arresting boys, provided they be of the small kind, and the reporters will have to laud their performances just as loyally as ever, or go without items.

---

*I have many such memories in my mind, but am thinking just at present of one particular one, where the Brannan Street butchers set their dogs on a Chinaman who was quietly passing with a basket of clothes on his head; and while the dogs mutilated his flesh, a butcher increased the hilarity of the occasion by knocking some of the Chinaman's teeth down his throat with half a brick. This incident sticks in my memory with a more malevolent tenacity, perhaps, on account of the fact that I was in the employ of a San Francisco journal at the time, and was not allowed to publish it because it might offend some of the peculiar element that subscribed for the paper.

The new form for local items in San Francisco will now be: "The ever-vigilant and efficient officer So-and-so succeeded, yesterday afternoon, in arresting Master Tommy Jones, after a determined resistance," etc., etc., followed by the customary statistics and final hurrah, with its unconscious sarcasm: "We are happy in being able to state that this is the forty-seventh boy arrested by this gallant officer since the new ordinance went into effect. The most extraordinary activity prevails in the police department. Nothing like it has been seen since we can remember."

The Private History of a Campaign That Failed

You have heard from a great many people who did something in the war; is it not fair and right that you listen a little moment to one who started out to do something in it, but didn't? Thousands entered the war, got just a taste of it, and then stepped out again permanently. These, by their very numbers, are respectable, and are therefore entitled to a sort of voice—not a loud one, but a modest one; not a boastful one, but an apologetic one. They ought not to be allowed much space among better people—people who did something. I grant that; but they ought at least to be allowed to state why they didn't do anything, and also to explain the process by which they didn't do anything. Surely this kind of light must have a sort of value.

Out West there was a good deal of confusion in men's minds during the first months of the great trouble—a good deal of unsettledness, of leaning first this way, then that, then the other way. It was hard for us to get our bearings. I call to mind an instance of this. I was piloting on the Mississippi when the news came that South Carolina had gone out of the Union on the 20th of December, 1860. My pilot mate was a New-Yorker. He was strong for the Union; so was I. But he would not listen to me with any patience; my loyalty was smirched, to his eye, because my father had owned slaves. I said, in palliation of this dark fact, that I had heard my father say, some years before he died, that

The Private History of a Campaign That Failed

slavery was a great wrong, and that he would free the solitary negro he then owned if he could think it right to give away the property of the family when he was so straitened in means. My mate retorted that a mere impulse was nothing—anybody could pretend impulse; and went on decrying my Unionism and libeling my ancestry. A month later the secession atmosphere had considerably thickened on the Lower Mississippi, and I became a rebel; so did he. We were together in New Orleans the 26th of January, when Louisiana went out of the Union. He did his full share of the rebel shouting, but was bitterly opposed to letting me do mine. He said that I came of bad stock—of a father who had been willing to set slaves free. In the following summer he was piloting a Federal gunboat and shouting for the Union again, and I was in the Confederate army. I held his note for some borrowed money. He was one of the most upright men I ever knew, but he repudiated that note without hesitation because I was a rebel and the son of a man who owned slaves.

In that summer—of 1861—the first wash of the wave of war broke upon the shores of Missouri. Our state was invaded by the Union forces. They took possession of St. Louis, Jefferson Barracks, and some other points. The Governor, Claib Jackson, issued his proclamation calling out fifty thousand militia to repel the invader.

I was visiting in the small town where my boyhood had been spent—Hannibal, Marion County. Several of us got together in a secret place by night and formed ourselves into a military company. One Tom Lyman, a young fellow of a good deal of spirit but of no military experience, was made captain; I was made second lieutenant. We had no first lieutenant; I do not know why; it was long ago. There were fifteen of us. By the advice of an innocent connected with the organization we called ourselves the Marion Rangers. I do not remember that any one found fault with the name. I did not; I thought it sounded quite well. The young fellow who proposed this title was perhaps a fair sample of the kind of stuff we were made of. He was young, ignorant, good-natured, well-meaning, trivial, full of romance, and given to reading chivalric novels and singing forlorn love-ditties. He had some pathetic little nickel-plated aristocratic instincts, and detested his name, which was Dunlap; detested it, partly because it was nearly as common in that region as Smith, but mainly because it had a plebeian sound to his ear. So he tried to ennoble it by writing it in this way: *d'Unlap.* That contented his eye, but left his ear unsatisfied, for people gave the new name the same old pronunciation—emphasis on the front end of it. He then did the bravest thing that can be imagined—a thing to make one shiver when one remembers how the world is given to resenting shams and affectations; he began to write his name so: *d'Un Lap.* And he waited patiently through the long storm of mud that was flung at this work of art, and he had his reward at last; for he lived to see that name accepted, and the emphasis put where he wanted it by people who had known him all his life, and to whom the tribe of Dunlaps had been as familiar as the rain and the sunshine for forty years. So sure of victory at last is the courage that can wait. He said he had found, by consulting some ancient French chronicles, that the name was rightly and originally written d'Un Lap; and said that if it were translated into English it would mean Peterson: *Lap,* Latin or Greek, he said, for stone or rock, same as the French *pierre,* that is to say, Peter: *d',* of or from; *un,* a or one; hence, d'Un Lap, of or from a stone or a Peter; that is to say, one who is the son of a stone, the son of a Peter—Peterson. Our militia company were not learned, and the explanation confused them; so they called him

Peterson Dunlap. He proved useful to us in his way; he named our camps for us, and he generally struck a name that was "no slouch," as the boys said.

That is one sample of us. Another was Ed Stevens, son of the town jeweler—trim-built, handsome, graceful, neat as a cat; bright, educated, but given over entirely to fun. There was nothing serious in life to him. As far as he was concerned, this military expedition of ours was simply a holiday. I should say that about half of us looked upon it in the same way; not consciously, perhaps, but unconsciously. We did not think; we were not capable of it. As for myself, I was full of unreasoning joy to be done with turning out of bed at midnight and four in the morning for a while; grateful to have a change, new scenes, new occupations, a new interest. In my thoughts that was as far as I went; I did not go into the details; as a rule, one doesn't at twenty-four.

Another sample was Smith, the blacksmith's apprentice. This vast donkey had some pluck, of a slow and sluggish nature, but a soft heart; at one time he would knock a horse down for some impropriety, and at another he would get homesick and cry. However, he had one ultimate credit to his account which some of us hadn't; he stuck to the war, and was killed in battle at last.

Jo Bowers, another sample, was a huge, good-natured, flax-headed lubber; lazy, sentimental, full of harmless brag, a grumbler by nature; an experienced, industrious, ambitious, and often quite picturesque liar, and yet not a successful one, for he had had no intelligent training, but was allowed to come up just any way. This life was serious enough to him, and seldom satisfactory. But he was a good fellow, anyway, and the boys all liked him. He was made orderly sergeant; Stevens was made corporal.

These samples will answer—and they are quite fair ones. Well, this herd of cattle started for the war. What could you expect of them? They did as well as they knew how; but, really, what was justly to be expected of them? Nothing, I should say. That is what they did.

We waited for a dark night, for caution and secrecy were necessary; then, toward midnight, we stole in couples and from various directions to the Griffith place, beyond the town; from that point we set out together on foot. Hannibal lies at the extreme southeastern corner of Marion County, on the Mississippi River; our objective point was the hamlet of New London, ten miles away, in Ralls County.

The first hour was all fun, all idle nonsense and laughter. But that could not be kept up. The steady trudging came to be like work; the play had somehow oozed out of it; the stillness of the woods and the somberness of the night began to throw a depressing influence over the spirits of the boys, and presently the talking died out and each person shut himself up in his own thoughts. During the last half of the second hour nobody said a word.

Now we approached a log farm-house where, according to report, there was a guard of five Union soldiers. Lyman called a halt; and there, in the deep gloom of the overhanging branches, he began to whisper a plan of assault upon that house, which made the gloom more depressing than it was before. It was a crucial moment; we realized, with a cold suddenness, that here was no jest—we were standing face to face with actual war. We were equal to the occasion. In our response there was no hesitation, no indecision: we said that if Lyman wanted to meddle with those soldiers, he could go ahead and do it; but if he waited for us to follow him, he would wait a long time.

Lyman urged, pleaded, tried to shame us, but it had no effect. Our course was plain, our minds were made up: we would flank the farm-house—go out around. And that was what we did.

We struck into the woods and entered upon a rough time, stumbling over roots, getting tangled in vines, and torn by briers. At last we reached an open place in a safe region, and sat down, blown and hot, to cool off and nurse our scratches and bruises. Lyman was annoyed, but the rest of us were cheerful; we had flanked the farm-house, we had made our first military movement, and it was a success; we had nothing to fret about, we were feeling just the other way. Horse-play and laughing began again; the expedition was become a holiday frolic once more.

Then we had two more hours of dull trudging and ultimate silence and depression; then, about dawn, we straggled into New London, soiled, heel-blistered, fagged with our little march, and all of us except Stevens in a sour and raspy humor and privately down on the war. We stacked our shabby old shotguns in Colonel Ralls's barn, and then went in a body and breakfasted with that veteran of the Mexican War. Afterward he took us to a distant meadow, and there in the shade of a tree we listened to an old-fashioned speech from him, full of gunpowder and glory, full of that adjective-piling, mixed metaphor and windy declamation which were regarded as eloquence in that ancient time and that remote region; and then he swore us on the Bible to be faithful to the State of Missouri and drive all invaders from her soil, no matter whence they might come or under what flag they might march. This mixed us considerably, and we could not make out just what service we were embarked in; but Colonel Ralls, the practised politician and phrase-juggler, was not similarly in doubt; he knew quite clearly that he had invested us in the cause of the Southern Confederacy. He closed the solemnities by belting around me the sword which his neighbor, Colonel Brown, had worn at Buena Vista and Molino del Rey; and he accompanied this act with another impressive blast.

Then we formed in line of battle and marched four miles to a shady and pleasant piece of woods on the border of the far-reaching expanses of a flowery prairie. It was an enchanting region for war—our kind of war.

We pierced the forest about half a mile, and took up a strong position, with some low, rocky, and wooded hills behind us, and a purling, limpid creek in front. Straightway half the command were in swimming and the other half fishing. The ass with the French name gave this position a romantic title, but it was too long, so the boys shortened and simplified it to Camp Ralls.

We occupied an old maple-sugar camp, whose half-rotted troughs were still propped against the trees. A long corn-crib served for sleeping-quarters for the battalion. On our left, half a mile away, were Mason's farm and house; and he was a friend to the cause. Shortly after noon the farmers began to arrive from several directions, with mules and horses for our use, and these they lent us for as long as the war might last, which they judged would be about three months. The animals were of all sizes, all colors, and all breeds. They were mainly young and frisky, and nobody in the command could stay on them long at a time; for we were town boys, and ignorant of horsemanship. The creature that fell to my share was a very small mule, and yet so quick and active that it could throw me without difficulty; and it did this whenever I got on it. Then it would bray—stretching its neck out, laying its ears back, and spreading its jaws till you could see down to its works. It was a disagreeable animal in every way. If I took it by the bridle and tried to lead it off the grounds, it would sit down and brace back, and no one could budge it. However, I was not entirely destitute of military resources, and I did presently manage to spoil this game; for I had seen many a steamboat aground in my time, and knew a trick or two which even a grounded mule would be obliged to respect. There was a well by the corn-crib; so I substituted thirty fathom of rope for the bridle, and fetched him home with the windlass.

I will anticipate here sufficiently to say that we did learn to ride, after some days' practice, but never well. We could not learn to like our animals; they were not choice ones, and most of them had annoying peculiarities of one kind or another. Stevens's horse would carry him, when he was not noticing, under the huge excrescences which form on the trunks of oak-trees, and wipe him out of the saddle; in this way Stevens got several bad hurts. Sergeant Bowers's horse was very large and tall, with slim, long legs, and looked like a railroad bridge. His size enabled him to reach all about, and as far as he wanted to, with his head; so he was always biting Bowers's legs. On the march, in the sun, Bowers slept a good deal; and as soon as the horse recognized that he was asleep he would reach around and bite him on the leg. His legs were black and blue with bites. This was the only thing that could ever make him swear, but this always did; whenever his horse bit him he always swore, and of course Stevens, who laughed at everything, laughed at this, and would even get into such convulsions over it as to lose his balance and fall off his horse; and then Bowers, already irritated by the pain of the horse-bite, would resent the laughter with hard language, and there would be a quarrel; so that horse made no end of trouble and bad blood in the command.

However, I will get back to where I was—our first afternoon in the sugar-camp. The sugar-troughs came very handy as horse-troughs, and we had plenty of corn to fill them with. I ordered Sergeant Bowers to feed my mule; but he said that if I reckoned he went to war to be a dry-nurse to a mule it wouldn't take me very long to find out my mistake. I believed that this was insubordination, but I was full of uncertainties about everything military, and so I let the thing pass, and went and ordered Smith, the blacksmith's apprentice, to feed the mule; but he merely gave me a large, cold, sarcastic grin, such as an ostensibly seven-year-old horse gives you when you lift his lip and find he is fourteen, and turned his back on me. I then went to the captain, and asked if it were not right and proper and military for me to have an orderly. He said it was, but as there was only one orderly in the corps, it was but right that he himself should have Bowers on his staff. Bowers said he wouldn't serve on anybody's staff; and if anybody thought he could make him, let him try it. So, of course, the thing had to be dropped; there was no other way.

Next, nobody would cook; it was considered a degradation; so we had no dinner. We lazied the rest of the pleasant afternoon away, some dozing under the trees, some smoking cob-pipes and talking sweethearts and war, some playing games. By late supper-time all hands were famished; and to meet the difficulty all hands turned to, on an equal footing, and gathered wood, built fires, and cooked the meal. Afterward everything was smooth for a while; then trouble broke out between the corporal and the sergeant, each claiming to rank the other. Nobody knew which was the higher office; so Lyman had to settle the matter by making the rank of both officers equal. The commander of an ignorant crew like that has many troubles and vexations which probably do not occur in the regular army at all. However, with the song-singing and yarn-spinning around the camp-fire, everything presently became serene again; and by and by we raked the corn down level in one end of the crib, and all went to bed on it, tying a horse to the door, so that he would neigh if any one tried to get in.*

We had some horsemanship drill every forenoon; then, afternoons, we rode off here and there in squads a few miles, and visited the farmers' girls, and had a youthful good time, and got an honest good dinner or supper, and then home again to camp, happy and content.

For a time life was idly delicious, it was perfect; there was nothing to mar it. Then came some farmers with an alarm one day. They said it was rumored that the enemy were advancing in our direction from over Hyde's prairie. The result was a sharp stir among us, and general consternation. It was a rude awakening from our pleasant trance. The rumor was but a rumor—nothing definite about it; so, in the confusion, we did not know which way to retreat. Lyman was for not retreating at all in these uncertain circumstances; but he found that if he tried to maintain that attitude he would fare badly, for the command were in no humor to put up with insubordination. So he yielded the point and called a council of war—to consist of himself and the three other officers; but the privates made such a fuss about being left out that we had to allow them to remain, for they were already present, and doing the most of the

---

*It was always my impression that that was what the horse was there for, and I know that it was also the impression of at least one other of the command, for we talked about it at the time, and admired the military ingenuity of the device; but when I was out West, three years ago, I was told by Mr. A. G. Fuqua, a member of our company, that the horse was his; that the leaving him tied at the door was a matter of mere forgetfulness, and that to attribute it to intelligent invention was to give him quite too much credit. In support of his position he called my attention to the suggestive fact that the artifice was not employed again. I had not thought of that before.

talking too. The question was, which way to retreat; but all were so flurried that nobody seemed to have even a guess to offer. Except Lyman. He explained in a few calm words that, inasmuch as the enemy were approaching from over Hyde's prairie, our course was simple: all we had to do was not to retreat *toward* him; any other direction would answer our needs perfectly. Everybody saw in a moment how true this was, and how wise; so Lyman got a great many compliments. It was now decided that we should fall back on Mason's farm.

It was after dark by this time, and as we could not know how soon the enemy might arrive, it did not seem best to try to take the horses and things with us; so we only took the guns and ammunition, and started at once. The route was very rough and hilly and rocky, and presently the night grew very black and rain began to fall; so we had a troublesome time of it, struggling and stumbling along in the dark; and soon some person slipped and fell, and then the next person behind stumbled over him and fell, and so did the rest, one after the other; and then Bowers came, with the keg of powder in his arms, while the command were all mixed together, arms and legs, on the muddy slope; and so he fell, of course, with the keg, and this started the whole detachment down the hill in a body, and they landed in the brook at the bottom in a pile, and each that was undermost pulling the hair and scratching and biting those that were on top of him; and those that were being scratched and bitten scratching and biting the rest in their turn, and all saying they would die before they would ever go to war again if they ever got out of this brook this time, and the invader might rot for all they cared, and the country along with him—and all such talk as that, which was dismal to hear and take part in, in such smothered, low voices, and such a grisly dark place and so wet, and the enemy, maybe, coming any moment. The keg of powder was lost, and the guns, too; so the growling and complaining continued straight along while the brigade pawed around the pasty hillside and slopped around in the brook hunting for these things; consequently we lost considerable time at this; and then we heard a sound, and held our breath and listened, and it seemed to be the enemy coming, though it could have been a cow, for it had a cough like a cow; but we did not wait, but left a couple of guns behind and struck out for Mason's again as briskly as we could scramble along in the dark. But we got lost presently among the rugged little ravines, and wasted a deal of time finding the way again, so it was after nine when we reached Mason's stile at last; then before we could open our mouths to give the countersign several dogs came bounding over the fence, with great riot and noise, and each of them took a soldier by the slack of his trousers and began to back away with him. We could not shoot the dogs without endangering the persons they were attached to; so we had to look on helpless at what was perhaps the most mortifying spectacle of the Civil War. There was light enough, and to spare, for the Masons had now run out on the porch with candles in their hands. The old man and his son came and undid the dogs without difficulty, all but Bowers's; but they couldn't undo his dog, they didn't know his combination; he was of the bull kind, and seemed to be set with a Yale time-lock; but they got him loose at last with some scalding water, of which Bowers got his share and returned thanks. Peterson Dunlap afterward made up a fine name for this engagement, and also for the night march which preceded it, but both have long ago faded out of my memory.

We now went into the house, and they began to ask us a world of questions, whereby it presently came out that we did not know anything concerning who or what we were running from; so the old gentleman made himself very frank, and said we were a curious breed of soldiers, and guessed we could be depended on to end up the war in time, because no government could stand the expense of the shoe-leather we should cost it trying to follow us around. "Marion *Rangers!* good name, b'gosh!" said he. And wanted to know why we hadn't had a picket-guard at the place where the road entered the prairie, and why we hadn't sent out a scouting party to spy out the enemy and bring us an account of his strength, and so on, before jumping up and stampeding out of a strong position upon a mere vague rumor—and so on, and so forth, till he made us all feel shabbier than the dogs had done, not half so enthusiastically welcome. So we went to bed shamed and low-spirited; except Stevens. Soon Stevens began to devise a garment for Bowers which could be made to automatically display his battle-scars to the grateful, or conceal them from the envious, according to his occasions; but Bowers was in no humor for this, so there was a fight, and when it was over Stevens had some battle-scars of his own to think about.

Then we got a little sleep. But after all we had gone through, our activities were not over for the night; for about two o'clock in the morning we heard a shout of warning from down the lane, accompanied by a chorus from all the dogs, and in a moment everybody was up and flying around to find out what the alarm was about. The alarmist was a horseman who gave notice that a detachment of Union soldiers was on its way from Hannibal with orders to capture and hang any bands like ours which it could find, and said we had no time to lose. Farmer Mason was in a flurry this time himself. He hurried us out of the house with all haste, and sent one of his negroes with us to show us where to hide ourselves and our telltale guns among the ravines half a mile away. It was raining heavily.

We struck down the lane, then across some rocky pastureland which offered good advantages for stumbling; consequently we were down in the mud most of the time, and every time a man went down he blackguarded the war, and the people that started it, and everybody connected with it, and gave himself the master dose of all for being so foolish as to go into it. At last we reached the wooded mouth of a ravine, and there we huddled ourselves under the streaming trees, and sent the negro back home. It was a dismal and heart-breaking time. We were like to be drowned with the rain, deafened with the howling wind and the booming thunder, and blinded by the lightning. It was, indeed, a wild night. The drenching we were getting was misery enough, but a deeper misery still was the reflection that the halter might end us before we were a day older. A death of this shameful sort had not occurred to us as being among the possibilities of war. It took the romance all out of the campaign, and turned our dreams of glory into a repulsive nightmare. As for doubting that so barbarous an order had been given, not one of us did that.

The long night wore itself out at last, and then the negro came to us with the news that the alarm had manifestly been a false one, and that breakfast would soon be ready. Straightway we were light-hearted again, and the world was bright, and life as full of hope and promise as ever—for we were young then. How long ago that was! Twenty-four years.

The mongrel child of philology named the night's refuge Camp Devastation, and no soul objected. The Masons gave us a Missouri country breakfast, in Missourian abundance, and we needed it: hot biscuits; hot "wheat bread," prettily criss-crossed in a lattice pattern on top; hot corn-pone; fried chicken; bacon, coffee, eggs, milk, buttermilk, etc.; and the world may be confidently challenged to furnish the equal of such a breakfast, as it is cooked in the South.

We stayed several days at Mason's; and after all these years the memory of the dullness, and stillness, and lifelessness of that slumberous farm-house still oppresses my spirit as with a sense of the presence of death and mourning. There was nothing to do, nothing to think about; there was no interest in life. The male part of the household were away in the fields all day, the women were busy and out of our sight; there was no sound but the plaintive wailing of a spinning-wheel, forever moaning out from some distant room—the most lonesome sound in nature, a sound steeped and sodden with homesickness and the emptiness of life. The family went to bed about dark every night, and as we were not invited to intrude any new customs we naturally followed theirs. Those nights were a hundred years long to youths accustomed to being up till twelve. We lay awake and miserable till that hour every time, and grew old and decrepit waiting through the still eternities for the clock-strikes. This was no place for town boys. So at last it was with something very like joy that we received news that the enemy were on our track again. With a new birth of the old warrior spirit we sprang to our places in line of battle and fell back on Camp Ralls.

Captain Lyman had taken a hint from Mason's talk, and he now gave orders that our camp should be guarded against surprise by the posting of pickets. I was ordered to place a picket at the forks of the road in Hyde's prairie. Night shut down black and threatening. I told Sergeant Bowers to go out to that place and stay till midnight; and, just as I was expecting, he said he wouldn't do it. I tried to get others to go, but all refused. Some excused themselves on account of the weather; but the rest were frank enough to say they wouldn't go in any kind of weather. This kind of thing sounds odd now, and impossible, but there was no surprise in it at the time. On the contrary, it seemed a perfectly natural thing to do. There were scores of little camps scattered over Missouri where the same thing was happening. These camps were composed of young men who had been born and reared to a sturdy independence, and who did not know what it meant to be ordered around by Tom, Dick, and Harry, whom they had known familiarly all their lives, in the village or on the farm. It is quite within the probabilities that this same thing was happening all over the South. James Redpath recognized the justice of this assumption, and furnished the following instance in support of it. During a short stay in East Tennessee he was in a citizen colonel's tent one day talking, when a big private appeared at the door, and, without salute or other circumlocution, said to the colonel:

"Say, Jim, I'm a-goin' home for a few days."

"What for?"

"Well, I hain't b'en there for a right smart while, and I'd like to see how things is comin' on."

"How long are you going to be gone?"

"'Bout two weeks."

"Well, don't be gone longer than that; and get back sooner if you can."

That was all, and the citizen officer resumed his conversation where the private had broken it off. This was in the first months of the war, of course. The camps in our part of Missouri were under Brigadier-General Thomas H. Harris. He was a townsman of ours, a first-rate fellow, and well liked; but we had all familiarly known him as the sole and modest-salaried operator in our telegraph-office, where he had to send about one despatch a week in ordinary times, and two when there was a rush of business; consequently, when he appeared in our midst one day, on the wing, and delivered a military command of some sort, in a large military fashion, nobody was surprised at the response which he got from the assembled soldiery:

"Oh, now, what'll you take to *don't*, Tom Harris?"

It was quite the natural thing. One might justly imagine that we were hopeless material for war. And so we seemed, in our ignorant state; but there were those among us who afterward learned the grim trade; learned to obey like machines; became valuable soldiers; fought all through the war, and came out at the end with excellent records. One of the very boys who refused to go on duty that night, and called me an ass for thinking he would expose himself to danger in such a foolhardy way, had become distinguished for intrepidity before he was a year older.

I did secure my picket that night—not by authority, but by diplomacy. I got Bowers to go by agreeing to exchange ranks with him for the time being, and go along and stand the watch with him as his subordinate. We stayed out there a couple of dreary hours in the pitchy darkness and the rain, with nothing to modify the dreariness but Bowers's monotonous growlings at the war and the weather; then we began to nod, and presently found it next to impossible to stay in the saddle; so we gave up the tedious job, and went back to the camp without waiting for the relief guard. We rode into camp without interruption or objection from anybody, and the enemy could have done the same, for there were no sentries. Everybody was asleep; at midnight there was nobody to send out another picket, so none was sent. We never tried to establish a watch at night again, as far as I remember, but we generally kept a picket out in the daytime.

The Private History of a Campaign That Failed

In that camp the whole command slept on the corn in the big corn-crib; and there was usually a general row before morning, for the place was full of rats, and they would scramble over the boys' bodies and faces, annoying and irritating everybody; and now and then they would bite some one's toe, and the person who owned the toe would start up and magnify his English and begin to throw corn in the dark. The ears were half as heavy as bricks, and when they struck they hurt. The persons struck would respond, and inside of five minutes every man would be locked in a death-grip with his neighbor. There was a grievous deal of blood shed in the corn-crib, but this was all that was spilt while I was in the war. No, that is not quite true. But for one circumstance it would have been all. I will come to that now.

Our scares were frequent. Every few days rumors would come that the enemy were approaching. In these cases we always fell back on some other camp of ours; we never stayed where we were. But the rumors always turned out to be false; so at last even we began to grow indifferent to them. One night a negro was sent to our corn-crib with the same old warning: the enemy was hovering in our neighborhood. We all said let him hover. We resolved to stay still and be comfortable. It was a fine warlike resolution, and no doubt we all felt the stir of it in our veins—for a moment. We had been having a very jolly time, that was full of horse-play and school-boy hilarity; but that cooled down now, and presently the fast-waning fire of forced jokes and forced laughs died out altogether, and the company became silent. Silent and nervous. And soon uneasy—worried—apprehensive. We had said we would stay, and we were committed. We could have been persuaded to go, but there was nobody brave enough to suggest it. An almost noiseless movement presently began in the dark by a general but unvoiced impulse. When the movement was completed each man knew that he was not the only person who had crept to the front wall and had his eye at a crack between the logs. No, we were all there; all there with our hearts in our throats, and staring out toward the sugar-troughs where the forest footpath came through. It was late, and there was a deep woodsy stillness everywhere. There was a veiled moonlight, which was only just strong enough to enable us to mark the general shape of objects. Presently a muffled sound caught our ears, and we recognized it as the hoof-beats of a horse or horses. And right away a figure appeared in the forest path; it could have been made of smoke, its mass had so little sharpness of outline. It was a man on horseback, and it seemed to me that there were others behind him. I got hold of a gun in the dark, and pushed it through a crack between the logs, hardly knowing what I was doing, I was so dazed with fright. Somebody said "Fire!" I pulled the trigger. I seemed to see a hundred flashes and hear a hundred reports, then I saw the man fall down out of the saddle. My first feeling was of surprised gratification; my first impulse was an apprentice-sportsman's impulse to run and pick up his game. Somebody said, hardly audibly, "Good—we've got him!—wait for the rest." But the rest did not come. We waited—listened—still no more came. There was not a sound, not the whisper of a leaf; just perfect stillness; an uncanny kind of stillness, which was all the more uncanny on account of the damp, earthy, late-night smells now rising and pervading it. Then, wondering, we crept stealthily out, and approached the man. When we got to him the moon revealed him distinctly. He was lying on his back, with his arms abroad; his mouth was open and his chest heaving with long gasps, and his white shirt-front was all splashed with blood. The thought shot through me that I was a murderer; that I had killed a man—a man who had never done me any harm. That was the coldest sensation that ever went through my marrow. I was down by him in a moment, helplessly stroking his forehead; and I would have given anything then—my own life freely—to make him again what he had been five minutes before. And all the boys seemed to be feeling in the same way; they hung over him, full of pitying interest, and tried all they could to help him, and said all sorts of regretful things. They had forgotten all about the enemy; they thought only of this one forlorn unit of the foe. Once my imagination persuaded me that the dying man gave me a reproachful look out of his shadowy eyes, and it seemed to me that I could rather he had stabbed me than done that. He muttered and mumbled like a dreamer in his sleep, about his wife and his child; and I thought with a new despair, "This thing that I have done does not end with him; it falls upon *them* too, and they never did me any harm, any more than he."

In a little while the man was dead. He was killed in war; killed in fair and legitimate war; killed in battle, as you may say; and yet he was as sincerely mourned by the opposing force as if he had been their brother. The boys stood there a half-hour sorrowing over him, and recalling the details of the tragedy, and wondering who he might be, and if he were a spy, and saying that if it were to do over again they would not hurt him unless he attacked them first. It soon came out that mine was not the only shot fired; there were five others—a division of the guilt which was a great relief to me, since it in some degree lightened and diminished the burden I was carrying. There were six shots fired at once; but I was not in my right mind at the time, and my heated imagination had magnified my one shot into a volley.

The man was not in uniform, and was not armed. He was a stranger in the country; that was all we ever found out about him. The thought of him got to preying upon me every night; I could not get rid of it. I could not drive it away, the taking of that unoffending life seemed such a wanton thing. And it seemed an epitome of war; that all war must be just that—the killing of strangers against whom you feel no personal animosity; strangers whom, in other circumstances, you would help if you found them in trouble, and who would help you if you needed it. My campaign was spoiled. It seemed to me that I was not rightly equipped for this awful business; that war was intended for men, and I for a child's nurse. I resolved to retire from this avocation of sham soldiership while I could save some remnant of my self-respect. These morbid thoughts clung to me against reason; for at bottom I did not believe I had touched that man. The law of probabilities decreed me guiltless of his blood; for in all my small experience with guns I had never hit anything I had tried to hit, and I knew I had done my best to hit him. Yet there was no solace in the thought. Against a diseased imagination, demonstration goes for nothing.

The rest of my war experience was of a piece with what I have already told of it. We kept monotonously falling back upon one camp or another, and eating up the country. I marvel now at the patience of the farmers and their families. They ought to have shot us; on the contrary, they were as hospitably kind and courteous to us as if we had deserved it. In one of these camps we found Ab Grimes, an Upper Mississippi pilot, who afterward became famous as a dare-devil rebel spy, whose career bristled with desperate adventures. The look and style of his comrades suggested that they had not come into the war to play, and their deeds made good the conjecture later. They were fine horsemen and good revolver shots; but their favorite arm was the lasso. Each had one at his pommel, and could snatch a man out of the saddle with it every time, on a full gallop, at any reasonable distance.

In another camp the chief was a fierce and profane old blacksmith of sixty, and he had furnished his twenty recruits with gigantic home-made bowie-knives, to be swung with the two hands, like the *machetes* of the Isthmus. It was a grisly spectacle to see that earnest band practising their murderous cuts and slashes under the eye of that remorseless old fanatic.

The last camp which we fell back upon was in a hollow near the village of Florida, where I was born—in Monroe County. Here we were warned one day, that a Union colonel was sweeping down on us with a whole regiment at his heel. This looked decidedly serious. Our boys went apart and consulted; then we went back and told the other companies present that the war was a disappointment to us and we were going to disband. They were getting ready themselves to fall back on some place or other, and we were only waiting for General Tom Harris, who expected to arrive at any moment; so they tried to persuade us to wait a little while, but the majority of us said no, we were accustomed to falling back, and didn't need any of Tom Harris's help; we could get along perfectly well without him—and save time, too. So about half of our fifteen, including myself, mounted and left on the instant; the others yielded to persuasion and stayed—stayed through the war.

An hour later we met General Harris on the road, with two or three people in his company—his staff, probably, but we could not tell; none of them were in uniform; uniforms had not come into vogue among us yet. Harris ordered us back; but we told him there was a Union colonel coming with a whole regiment in his wake, and it looked as if there was going to be a disturbance; so we had concluded to go home. He raged a little, but it was of no use; our minds were made up. We had done our share; had killed one man, exterminated one army, such as it was; let him go and kill the rest, and that would end the war. I did not see that brisk young general again until last year; then he was wearing white hair and whiskers.

In time I came to know that Union colonel whose coming frightened me out of the war and crippled the Southern cause to that extent—General Grant. I came within a few hours of seeing him when he was as unknown as I was myself; at a time when anybody could have said, "Grant?—Ulysses S. Grant? I do not remember hearing the name before." It seems difficult to realize that there was once a time when such a remark could be rationally made; but there *was*, and I was within a few miles of the place and the occasion, too, though proceeding in the other direction.

The thoughtful will not throw this war paper of mine lightly aside as being valueless. It has this value: it is a not unfair picture of what went on in many and many a militia camp in the first months of the rebellion, when the green recruits were without discipline, without the steadying and heartening influence of trained leaders: when all their circumstances were new and strange, and charged with exaggerated terrors, and before the invaluable experience of actual collision in the field had turned them from rabbits into soldiers. If this side of the picture of that early day has not before been put into history, then history has been to that degree incomplete, for it had and has its rightful place there. There was more Bull Run material scattered through the early camps of this country than exhibited itself at Bull Run. And yet it learned its trade presently, and helped to fight the great battles later. I could have become a soldier myself if I had waited. I had got part of it learned; I knew more about retreating than the man that invented retreating.

V.

RELIGION AND THE MORAL ORDER

About Smells

In a recent issue of the "Independent," the Rev. T. De Witt Talmage, of Brooklyn, has the following utterance on the subject of "Smells":

> I have a good Christian friend who, if he sat in the front pew in church, and a working man should enter the door at the other end, would smell him instantly. My friend is not to blame for the sensitiveness of his nose, any more than you would flog a pointer for being keener on the scent than a stupid watch-dog. The fact is, if you had all the churches free, by reason of the mixing up of the common people with the uncommon, you would keep one-half of Christendom sick at their stomach. If you are going to kill the church thus with bad smells, I will have nothing to do with this work of evangelization.

We have reason to believe that there will be laboring men in heaven; and also a number of negroes, and Esquimaux, and Tierra del Fuegans, and Arabs, and a few Indians, and possibly even some Spaniards and Portuguese. All things are possible with God. We shall have all these sorts of people in heaven; but, alas! in getting them we shall lose the society of Dr. Talmage. Which is to say, we shall lose the company of one who could give more real "tone" to celestial society than any other contribution Brooklyn could furnish. And what would eternal happiness be without the Doctor? Blissful, unquestionably—we know that well enough—but would it be *distingué*, would it be *recherché* without him? St. Matthew without stockings or sandals; St. Jerome bareheaded, and with a coarse brown blanket robe dragging the ground; St. Sebastian with scarcely any raiment at all—these we should see, and should enjoy seeing them; but would we not miss a spike-tailed coat and kids, and turn away regretfully, and say to parties from the Orient: "These are well enough, but you ought to see Talmage of Brooklyn." I fear me that in the better world we shall not even have Dr. Talmage's "good Christian friend." For if he were sitting under the glory of the Throne, and the keeper of the keys admitted a Benjamin Franklin or other laboring man, that "friend," with his fine natural powers infinitely augmented by emancipation from hampering flesh, would detect him with a single sniff, and immediately take his hat and ask to be excused.

To all outward seeming, the Rev. T. De Witt Talmage is of the same material as that used in the construction of his early predecessors in the ministry; and yet one feels that there must be a difference somewhere between him and the Savior's first disciples. It may be because here, in the nineteenth century, Dr. T. has had advantages which Paul and Peter and the others could not and did not have. There was a lack of polish about them, and a looseness of etiquette, and a want of exclusiveness, which one cannot help noticing. They healed the very beggars, and held intercourse with people of a villainous odor every day. If the subject of these remarks had been chosen among the original Twelve Apostles, he would not have associated with the rest, because he could not have stood the fishy smell of some of his comrades who came from around the Sea of Galilee. He would have resigned his commission with some such remark as he makes in the extract quoted above: "Master, if thou art going to kill the church thus with bad smells, I will have nothing to do with this work of evangelization." He is a disciple, and makes that remark to the Master; the only difference is, that he makes it in the nineteenth instead of the first century.

Is there a choir in Mr. T.'s church? And does it ever occur that they have no better manners than to sing that hymn which is so suggestive of laborers and mechanics:

> "*Son of the Carpenter! receive*
> *This humble work of mine?*"

Now, can it be possible that in a handful of centuries the Christian character has fallen away from an imposing heroism that scorned even the stake, the cross, and the axe, to a poor little effeminacy that withers and wilts under an unsavory smell? We are not prepared to believe so, the reverend Doctor and his friend to the contrary notwithstanding.

REFLECTIONS ON THE SABBATH

The day of rest comes but once a week, and sorry am I that it does not come oftener. Man is so constituted that he can stand more rest than this. I often think regretfully that it would have been so easy to have two Sundays in a week, and yet it was not so ordained. The omnipotent Creator could have made the world in three days just as easily as he made it in six, and this would have doubled the Sundays. Still it is not our place to criticise the wisdom of the Creator. When we feel a depraved inclination to question the judgment of Providence in stacking up double eagles in the coffers of Michael Reese and leaving better men to dig for a livelihood, we ought to stop and consider that we are not expected to help order things, and so drop the subject. If allpowerful Providence grew weary after six days' labor, such worms as we are might reasonably expect to break down in three, and so require two Sundays—but as I said before, it ill becomes us to hunt up flaws in matters which are so far out of our jurisdiction. I hold that no man can meddle with the exclusive affairs of Providence and offer suggestions for their improvement, without making himself in a manner conspicuous. Let us take things as we find them—though, I am free to confess, it goes against the grain to do it, sometimes.

What put me in this religious train of mind, was attending church at Dr. Wadsworth's this morning. I had not been to church before for many months, because I never could get a pew, and therefore had to sit in the gallery, among the sinners. I stopped that because my proper place was down among the elect, inasmuch as I was brought up a Presbyterian, and consider myself a brevet member of Dr. Wadsworth's church. I always was a brevet. I was sprinkled in infancy, and look upon that as conferring the rank of Brevet Presbyterian. It affords none of the emoluments of the Regular Church—simply confers honorable rank upon the recipient and the right to be punished as a Presbyterian hereafter; that is, the substantial Presbyterian punishment of fire and brimstone instead of this heterodox hell of remorse of conscience of these blamed wildcat religions. The heaven and hell of the wildcat religions are vague and ill defined but there is nothing mixed about the Presbyterian heaven and hell. The Presbyterian hell is all misery; the heaven all happiness—nothing to do. But when a man dies on a wildcat basis, he will never rightly know hereafter which department he is in—but he will think he is in hell anyhow, no matter which place he goes to; because in the good place they pro-gress, pro-gress, pro-gress—study, study, study, all the time—and if this isn't hell I don't know what is; and in the bad place he will be worried by the remorse of conscience. Their bad place is preferable, though, because eternity is long, and before a man got half through it he would forget what it was he had been so sorry about. Naturally he would then become cheerful again; but the party who went to heaven would go on progressing and progressing, and studying and studying until he would finally get discouraged and wish he were in hell, where he wouldn't require such a splendid education.

Dr. Wadsworth never fails to preach an able sermon; but every now and then, with an admirable assumption of not being aware of it, he will get off a firstrate joke and then frown severely at any one who is surprised into smiling at it. This is not fair. It is like throwing a bone to a dog and then arresting him with a look just as he is going to seize it. Several people there on Sunday suddenly laughed and as suddenly stopped again, when he gravely gave the Sunday school books a blast and spoke of "the good little boys in them who always went to Heaven, and the bad little boys who infallibly got drowned on Sunday," and then swept a savage frown around the house and blighted every smile in the congregation.

How I Became Interested in Satan

When I was a Sunday-school scholar, something more than sixty years ago, I became interested in Satan, and wanted to find out all I could about him. I began to ask questions, but my class-teacher, Mr. Barclay, the stonemason, was reluctant about answering them, it seemed to me. I was anxious to be praised for turning my thoughts to serious subjects when there wasn't another boy in the village who could be hired to do such a thing. I was greatly interested in the incident of Eve and the serpent, and thought Eve's calmness was perfectly noble. I asked Mr. Barclay if he had ever heard of another woman who, being approached by a serpent, would not excuse herself and break for the nearest timber. He did not answer my question, but rebuked me for inquiring into matters above my age and comprehension. I will say for Mr. Barclay that he was willing to tell me the facts of Satan's history, but he stopped there: he wouldn't allow any discussion of them.

In the course of time we exhausted the facts. There were only five or six of them; you could set them all down on a visiting-card. I was disappointed. I had been meditating a biography, and was grieved to find that there were no materials. I said as much, with the tears running down. Mr. Barclay's sympathy and compassion were aroused, for he was a most kind and gentle-spirited man, and he patted me on the head and cheered me up by saying there was a whole vast ocean of materials! I can still feel the happy thrill which these blessed words shot through me.

Then he began to bail out that ocean's riches for my encouragement and joy. Like this: it was "conjectured"—though not established—that Satan was originally an angel in heaven; that he fell; that he rebelled, and brought on a war; that he was defeated, and banished to perdition. Also, "we have reason to believe" that later he did so-and-so; that "we are warranted in supposing" that at a subsequent time he traveled extensively, seeking whom he might devour; that a couple of centuries afterward, "as tradition instructs us," he took up the cruel trade of tempting people to their ruin, with vast and fearful results; that by and by, "as the probabilities seem to indicate," he may have done certain things, he might have done certain other things, he must have done still other things.

And so on and so on. We set down the five known facts by themselves, on a piece of paper, and numbered it "page 1"; then on fifteen hundred other pieces of paper we set down the "conjectures," and "suppositions," and "maybes," and "perhapses," and "doubtlesses," and "rumors," and "guesses," and "probabilities," and "likelihoods," and "we are permitted to thinks," and "we are warranted in believings," and "might have beens," and "could have beens," and "must have beens," and "unquestionablys," and "without a shadow of doubts"—and behold!

Materials? Why, we had enough to build a biography of Shakespeare!

Yet he made me put away my pen; he would not let me write the history of Satan. Why? Because, as he said, he had suspicions—suspicions that my attitude in this matter was not reverent, and that a person must be reverent when writing about the sacred characters. He said any one who spoke flippantly of Satan would be frowned upon by the religious world and also be brought to account. I assured him, in earnest and sincere words, that he had wholly misconceived my attitude; that I had the highest respect for Satan, and that my reverence for him equaled, and possibly even exceeded, that of any member of any church. I said it wounded me deeply to perceive by his words that he thought I would make fun of Satan, and deride him, laugh at him, scoff at him; whereas in truth I had never thought of such a thing, but had only a warm desire to make fun of those others and laugh at *them*. "What others?" "Why, the Supposers, the Perhapsers, the Might-Have-Beeners, the Could-Have-Beeners, the Must-Have-Beeners, the Without-a-Shadow-of-Doubters, the We-Are-Warranted-in-Believingers, and all that funny crop of solemn architects who have taken a good solid foundation of five indisputable and unimportant facts and built upon it a Conjectural Satan thirty miles high."

What did Mr. Barclay do then? Was he disarmed? Was he silenced? No. He was shocked. He was so shocked that he visibly shuddered. He said the Satanic Traditioners and Perhapsers and Conjecturers were *themselves* sacred! As sacred as their work. So sacred that whoso ventured to mock them or make fun of their work, could not afterward enter any respectable house, even by the back door.

How true were his words, and how wise! How fortunate it would have been for me if I had heeded them. But I was young, I was but seven years of age, and vain, foolish, and anxious to attract attention. I wrote the biography, and have never been in a respectable house since.

Theoretical and Practical Morals

It has always been difficult—leave that word difficult—not exceedingly difficult, but just difficult, nothing more than that, not the slightest shade to add to that—just difficult—to respond properly, in the right phraseology, when compliments are paid to me; but it is more than difficult when the compliments are paid to a better than I—my wife.

And while I am not here to testify against myself—I can't be expected to do so, a prisoner in your own country is not admitted to do so—as to which member of the family wrote my books, I could say in general that really I wrote the books myself. My wife puts the facts in, and they make it respectable. My modesty won't suffer while compliments are being paid to literature, and through literature to my family. I can't get enough of them.

I am curiously situated to-night. It so rarely happens that I am introduced by a humorist; I am generally introduced by a person of grave walk and carriage. That makes the proper background of gravity for brightness. I am going to alter to suit, and haply I may say some humorous things.

When you start with a blaze of sunshine and upburst of humor, when you begin with that, the proper office of humor is to reflect, to put you into that pensive mood of deep thought, to make you think of your sins, if you wish half an hour to fly. Humor makes me reflect now to-night, it sets the thinking machinery in motion. Always, when I am thinking, there come suggestions of what I am, and what we all are, and what we are coming to. A sermon comes from my lips always when I listen to a humorous speech.

I seize the opportunity to throw away frivolities, to say something to plant the seed, and make all better than when I came. In Mr. Grossmith's remarks there was a subtle something suggesting my favorite theory of the difference between theoretical morals and practical morals. I try to instil practical morals in the place of theatrical—I mean theoretical; but as an addendum—an annex—something added to theoretical morals.

When your chairman said it was the first time he had ever taken the chair, he did not mean that he had not taken lots of other things; he attended my first lecture and took notes. This indicated the man's disposition. There was nothing else flying round, so he took notes; he would have taken anything he could get.

I can bring a moral to bear here which shows the difference between theoretical morals and practical morals. Theoretical morals are the sort you get on your mother's knee, in good books, and from the pulpit. You gather them in your head, and not in your heart; they are theory without practice. Without the assistance of practice to perfect them, it is difficult to teach a child to "be honest, don't steal."

I will teach you how it should be done, lead you into temptation, teach you how to steal, so that you may recognize when you have stolen and feel the proper pangs. It is no good going round and bragging you have never taken the chair.

As by the fires of experience, so by commission of crime, you learn real morals. Commit all the crimes, familiarize yourself with all sins, take them in rotation (there are only two or three thousand of them), stick to it, commit two or three every day, and by-and-by you will be proof against them. When you are through you will be proof against all sins and morally perfect. You will be vaccinated against every possible commission of them. This is the only way.

I will read you a written statement upon the subject that I wrote three years ago to read to the Sabbath-schools. No! I have left it at home. Still, it was a mere statement of fact, illustrating the value of practical morals produced by the commission of crime.

It was in my boyhood—just a statement of fact, reading is only more formal, merely facts, merely pathetic facts, which I can state so as to be understood. It relates to the first time I ever stole a watermelon; that is, I think it was the first time; anyway, it was right along there somewhere.

I stole it out of a farmer's wagon while he was waiting on another customer. "Stole" is a harsh term. I withdrew—I retired that watermelon. I carried it to a secluded corner of a lumber-yard. I broke it open. It was green—the greenest watermelon raised in the valley that year.

The minute I saw it was green I was sorry, and began to reflect—reflection is the beginning of reform. If you don't reflect when you commit a crime then that crime is of no use; it might just as well have been committed by someone else. You must reflect or the value is lost; you are not vaccinated against committing it again.

I began to reflect. I said to myself: "What ought a boy to do who has stolen a green watermelon? What would George Washington do, the father of his country, the only American who could not tell a lie? What would he do? There is only one right, high, noble thing for any boy to do who has stolen a watermelon of that class: he must make restitution; he must restore that stolen property to its rightful owner." I said I would do it when I made that good resolution. I felt it to be a noble, uplifting obligation. I rose up spiritually stronger and refreshed. I carried that watermelon back—

what was left of it—and restored it to the farmer, and made him give me a ripe one in its place.

Now you see that this constant impact of crime upon crime protects you against further commission of crime. It builds you up. A man can't become morally perfect by stealing one or a thousand green watermelons, but every little helps.

I was at a great school yesterday (St. Paul's), where for four hundred years they have been busy with brains, and building up England by producing Pepys, Miltons, and Marlboroughs. Six hundred boys left to nothing in the world but theoretical morality. I wanted to become the professor of practical morality, but the high master was away, so I suppose I shall have to go on making my living the same old way—by adding practical to theoretical morality.

What are the glory that was Greece, the grandeur that was Rome, compared to the glory and grandeur and majesty of a perfected morality such as you see before you?

The New Vagabonds are old vagabonds (undergoing the old sort of reform). You drank my health; I hope I have not been unuseful. Take this system of morality to your hearts. Take it home to your neighbors and your graves, and I hope that it will be a long time before you arrive there.

Journey to Damascus*

Properly, with the sorry relics we bestrode, it was a three days' journey to Damascus. It was necessary that we should do it in less than two. It was necessary because our three pilgrims would not travel on the Sabbath day. We were all perfectly willing to keep the Sabbath day, but there are times when to keep the *letter* of a sacred law whose spirit is righteous, becomes a sin, and this was a case in point. We pleaded for the tired, ill-treated horses, and tried to show that their faithful service deserved kindness in return and their hard lot compassion. But when did ever self-righteousness know the sentiment of pity? What were a few long hours added to the hardships of some overtaxed brutes when weighed against the peril of those human souls? It was not the most promising party to travel with and hope to gain a higher veneration for religion through the example of its devotees. We said the Saviour, who pitied dumb beasts and taught that the ox must be rescued from the mire even on the Sabbath day, would not have counseled a forced march like this. We said the "long trip" was exhausting and therefore dangerous in the blistering heats of summer, even when the ordinary day's stages were traversed, and if we persisted in this hard march, some of us might be stricken down with the fevers of the country in consequence of it. Nothing could move the pilgrims. They

*Editor's title.

must press on. Men might die, horses might die, but they must enter upon holy soil next week, with no Sabbath-breaking stain upon them. Thus they were willing to commit a sin against the spirit of religious law in order that they might preserve the letter of it. It was not worthwhile to tell them "the letter kills." I am talking now about personal friends, men whom I like, men who are good citizens, who are honorable, upright, conscientious; but whose idea of the Saviour's religion seems to me distorted. They lecture our short-comings unsparingly, and every night they call us together and read to us chapters from the Testament that are full of gentleness, of charity, and of tender mercy; and then all the next day they stick to their saddles clear up to the summits of these rugged mountains, and clear down again. Apply the Testament's gentleness and charity and tender mercy to a toiling, worn and weary horse? Nonsense—these are for God's human creatures, not his dumb ones. What the pilgrims choose to do, respect for their almost sacred character demands that I should allow to pass—but I would so like to catch any other member of the party riding his horse up one of these exhausting hills once!

We have given the pilgrims a good many examples that might benefit them, but it is virtue thrown away. They have never heard a cross word out of our lips toward each other—but *they* have quarreled once or twice. We love to hear them at it after they have been lecturing us. The very first thing they did, coming ashore at Beirut, was to quarrel in the boat. I have said I like them, and I do like them—but every time they read me a scorcher of a lecture I mean to talk back in print.

Not content with doubling the legitimate stages, they switched off the main road and went away out of the way to visit an absurd fountain called Figia, because Baalam's ass had drank there once. So we journeyed on, through the terrible hills and deserts and the roasting sun, and then far into the night, seeking the honored pool of Baalam's ass, the patron saint of all Pilgrims like us. I find no entry but this in my notebook:

> Rode today, all together thirteen hours, through deserts partly, and partly over barren, unsightly hills, and latterly through wild, rocky scenery, and camped at about eleven o'clock at night on the banks of a limpid stream, near a Syrian village. Do not know its name—do not wish to know it—want to go to bed. Two horses lame (mine and Jack's) and the others worn out. Jack and I walked three or four miles over the hills and led the horses. Fun—but of a mild type.

Twelve or thirteen hours in the saddle, even in a Christian land and a Christian climate, and on a good horse, is a tiresome journey; but in an oven like Syria, in a ragged spoon of a saddle that slips fore-and-aft, and "thort-ships," and every way, and on a horse that is tired and lame and yet must be whipped and spurred with hardly a moment's cessation all day long, till the blood comes from his side, and your conscience hurts you every time you strike if you are half a man—it is a journey to be remembered in bitterness of spirit and execrated with emphasis for a liberal division of a man's lifetime.

As Concerns Interpreting the Diety

I

This line of hieroglyphs was for fourteen years the despair of all the scholars who labored over the mysteries of the Rosetta stone:

After five years of study Champollion translated it thus:

> Therefore let the worship of Epiphanes be maintained in all the temples, this upon pain of death.

That was the twenty-fourth translation that had been furnished by scholars. For a time it stood. But only for a time. Then doubts began to assail it and undermine it, and the scholars resumed their labors. Three years of patient work produced eleven new translations; among them, this, by Grunfeldt, was received with considerable favor:

> The horse of Epiphanes shall be maintained at the public expense; this upon pain of death.

But the following rendering, by Gospodin, was received by the learned world with yet greater favor:

145

> The priest shall explain the wisdom of Epiphanes to all these people, and these shall listen with reverence, upon pain of death.

Seven years followed, in which twenty-one fresh and widely varying renderings were scored—none of them quite convincing. But now, at last, came Rawlinson, the youngest of all the scholars, with a translation which was immediately and universally recognized as being the correct version, and his name became famous in a day. So famous, indeed, that even the children were familiar with it; and such a noise did the achievement itself make that not even the noise of the monumental political event of that same year—the flight from Elba—was able to smother it to silence. Rawlinson's version reads as follows:

> Therefore, walk not away from the wisdom of Epiphanes, but turn and follow it; so shall it conduct thee to the temple's peace, and soften for thee the sorrows of life and the pains of death.

Here is another difficult text:

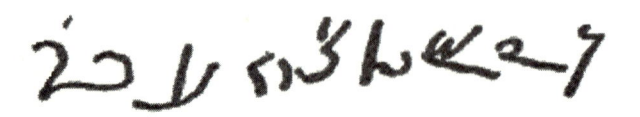

It is demotic—a style of Egyptian writing and a phase of the language which has perished from the knowledge of all men twenty-five hundred years before the Christian era.

Our red Indians have left many records, in the form of pictures, upon our crags and boulders. It has taken our most gifted and painstaking students two centuries to get at the meanings hidden in these pictures; yet there are still two little lines of hieroglyphics among the figures grouped upon the Dighton Rocks which they have not succeeded in interpreting to their satisfaction. These:

The suggested solutions are practically innumerable; they would fill a book.

Thus we have infinite trouble in solving man-made mysteries; it is only when we set out to discover the secret of God that our difficulties disappear. It was always so. In antique Roman times it was the custom of the Deity to try to conceal His intentions in the entrails of birds, and this was patiently and hopefully continued century after century, although the attempted concealment never succeeded, in a single recorded instance. The augurs could read entrails as easily as a modern child can read coarse print. Roman history is full of the marvels of interpretation which these extraordinary men performed. These strange and wonderful achievements move our awe and compel our admiration. Those men could pierce to the marrow of a mystery instantly. If the Rosetta-stone idea had been introduced it would have defeated them, but entrails had no embarrassments for them. Entrails have gone out, now—entrails and dreams. It was at last found out that as hiding-places for the divine intentions they were inadequate.

A part of the wall of Valletri in former times been struck with thunder, the response of the soothsayers was, that a native of that town would some time or other arrive at supreme power.—*Bohn's Suetonius,* p. 138.

"Some time or other." It looks indefinite, but no matter, it happened, all the same; one needed only to wait, and be patient, and keep watch, then he would find out that the thunder-stroke had Caesar Augustus in mind, and had come to give notice.

There were other advance-advertisements. One of them appeared just before Caesar Augustus was born, and was most poetic and touching and romantic in its feelings and aspects. It was a dream. It was dreamed by Caesar Augustus's mother, and interpreted at the usual rates:

> Atia, before her delivery, dreamed that her bowels stretched to the stars and expanded through the whole circuit of heaven and earth.—*Suetonius,* p. 139.

That was in the augur's line, and furnished him no difficulties, but it would have taken Rawlinson and Champollion fourteen years to make sure of what it meant, because they would have been surprised and dizzy. It would have been too late to be valuable, then, and the bill for service would have been barred by the statute of limitation.

In those old Roman days a gentleman's education was not complete until he had taken a theological course at the seminary and learned how to translate entrails. Caesar Augustus's education received this final polish. All through his life, whenever he had poultry on the menu he saved the interiors and kept himself informed of the Deity's plans by exercising upon those interiors the arts of augury.

> In his first consulship, while he was observing the auguries, twelve vultures presented themselves, as they

had done to Romulus. And when he offered sacrifice, the livers of all the victims were folded inward in the lower part; a circumstance which was regarded by those present who had skill in things of that nature, as an indubitable prognostic of great and wonderful fortune.—*Suetonius*, p. 141.

"Indubitable" is a strong word, but no doubt it was justified, if the livers were really turned that way. In those days chicken livers were strangely and delicately sensitive to coming events, no matter how far off they might be; and they could never keep still, but would curl and squirm like that, particularly when vultures came and showed interest in that approaching great event and in breakfast.

II

We may now skip eleven hundred and thirty or forty years, which brings us down to enlightened Christian times and the troubled days of King Stephen of England. The augur has had his day and has been long ago forgotten; the priest had fallen heir to his trade.

King Henry is dead; Stephen, that bold and outrageous person, comes flying over from Normandy to steal the throne from Henry's daughter. He accomplished his crime, and Henry of Huntington, a priest of high degree, mourns over it in his Chronicle. The Archbishop of Canterbury consecrated Stephen: "wherefore the Lord visited the Archbishop with the same judgment which he had inflicted upon him who struck Jeremiah the great priest: he died within a year."

Stephen's was the greater offense, but Stephen could wait; not so the Archbishop, apparently.

The kingdom was a prey to intestine wars; slaughter, fire, and rapine spread ruin throughout the land; cries of distress, horror, and woe rose in every quarter.

That was the result of Stephen's crime. These unspeakable conditions continued during nineteen years. Then Stephen died as comfortably as any man ever did, and was honorably buried. It makes one pity the poor Archbishop, and with that he, too, could have been let off as leniently. How did Henry of Huntington know that the Archbishop was sent to his grave by judgment of God for consecrating Stephen? He does not explain. Neither does he explain why Stephen was awarded a pleasanter death than he was entitled to, while the aged King Henry, his predecessor, who had ruled England thirty-five years to the people's strongly worded satisfaction, was condemned to close his life in circumstances most distinctly unpleasant, inconvenient, and disagreeable. His was probably the most uninspiring funeral that is set down in history. There is not a detail about it that is attractive. It seems to have been just the funeral for Stephen, and even at this far-distant day it is matter of just regret that by an indiscretion the wrong man got it.

Whenever God punishes a man, Henry of Huntington knows why it was done, and tells us; and his pen is eloquent with admiration; but when a man has earned punishment, and escapes, he does not explain. He is evidently puzzled, but he does not say anything. I think it is often apparent that he is pained by these discrepancies, but loyally tries his best not to show it. When he cannot praise, he delivers himself of a silence so marked that a suspicious person could mistake it for suppressed criticism. However, he has plenty of opportunities to feel contented with the way things go—his book is full of them.

As Concerns Interpreting the Deity 151

King David of Scotland . . . under color of religion caused his followers to deal most barbarously with the English. They ripped open women, tossed children on the points of spears, butchered priests at the altars, and, cutting off the heads from the images on crucifixes, placed them on the bodies of the slain, while in exchange they fixed on the crucifixes the heads of their victims. Wherever the Scots came, there was the same scene of horror and cruelty: women shrieking, old men lamenting, amid the groans of the dying and the despair of the living.

But the English got the victory.

Then the chief of the men of Lothian fell, pierced by an arrow, and all his followers were put to flight. For the Almighty was offended at them and their strength was rent like a cobweb.

Offended at them for what? For committing those fearful butcheries? No, for that was the common custom on both sides, and not open to criticism. Then was it for doing the butcheries "under cover of religion"? No, that was not it; religious feeling was often expressed in that fervent way all through those old centuries. The truth is, He was not offended at "them" at all; He was only offended at their king, who had been false to an oath. Then why did not He put the punishment upon the king instead of upon "them"? It is a difficult question. One can see by the Chronicle that the "judgments" fell rather customarily upon the wrong person, but Henry of Huntington does not explain why. Here is one that went true; the chronicler's satisfaction in it is not hidden:

> In the month of August, Providence displayed its justice in a remarkable manner; for two of the nobles who had converted monasteries into fortifications, expelling the monks, their sin being the same, met with a similar punishment. Robert Marmion was one, Godfrey de Mandeville the other. Robert Marmion, issuing forth against the enemy, was slain under the walls of the monastery, being the only one who fell, though he was surrounded by his troops. Dying excommunicated, he became subject to death everlasting. In like manner Earl Godfrey was singled out among his followers, and shot with an arrow by a common foot-soldier. He made light of the wound, but he died of it in a few days, under excommunication. See here the like judgment of God, memorable through all ages!

The exaltation jars upon me; not because of the death of the men, for they deserved that, but because it is death eternal, in white-hot fire and flame. It makes my flesh crawl. I have not known more than three men, or perhaps four, in my whole lifetime, whom I would rejoice to see writhing in those fires for even a year, let alone forever. I believe I would relent before the year was up, and get them out if I could. I think that in the long run, if a man's wife and babies, who had not harmed me, should come crying and pleading, I couldn't stand it; I know I should forgive him and let him go, even if he had violated a monastery. Henry of Huntington has been watching Godfrey and Marmion for nearly seven hundred and fifty years, now, but I couldn't do it, I know I couldn't. I am soft and gentle in my nature, and I should have forgiven them seventy-and-seven times, long ago. And I think God has; but this is only an opinion, and not authoritative, like Henry of Huntington's interpretations. I could learn to interpret, but I have never tried; I get so little time.

All through his book Henry exhibits his familiarity with the intentions of God, and with the reasons for his intentions. Sometimes—very often, in fact—the act follows the intention after such a wide interval of time that one wonders how Henry could fit one act out of a hundred to one intention out of a hundred and get the thing right every time when there was such abundant choice among acts and intentions. Sometimes a man offends the Deity with a crime, and is punished for it thirty years later; meantime he has committed a million other crimes: no matter, Henry can pick out the one that brought the worms. Worms were generally used in those days for the slaying of particularly wicked people. This has gone out, now, but in old times it was a favorite. It always indicated a case of "wrath." For instance:

> ... the just God avenging Robert Fitzhilderbrand's perfidy, a worm grew in his vitals, which gradually gnawing its way through his intestines fattened on the abandoned man till, tortured with excruciating sufferings and venting himself in bitter moans, he was by a fitting punishment brought to his end.—p. 400.

It was probably an alligator, but we cannot tell; we only know it was a particular breed, and only used to convey wrath. Some authorities think it was an ichthyosaurus, but there is much doubt.

However, one thing we do know; and that is that that worm had been due years and years. Robert F. had violated a monastery once; he had committed unprintable crimes since, and they had been permitted—under disapproval—

but the ravishment of the monastery had not been forgotten nor forgiven, and the worm came at last.

Why were these reforms put off in this strange way? What was to be gained by it? Did Henry of Huntington really know his facts, or was he only guessing? Sometimes I am half persuaded that he is only a guesser, and not a good one. The divine wisdom must surely be of the better quality than he makes it out to be.

Five hundred years before Henry's time some forecasts of the Lord's purposes were furnished by a pope, who perceived, by certain perfectly trustworthy signs furnished by the Deity for the information of His familiars, that the end of the world was

> ... about to come. But as this end of the world draws near many things are at hand which have not before happened, as changes in the air, terrible signs in the heavens, tempests out of the common order of the seasons, wars, famines, pestilences, earthquakes in various places; all which will not happen in our days, but after our days all will come to pass.

Still, the end was so near that these signs were "sent before that we may be careful for our souls and be found prepared to meet the impending judgment."

That was thirteen hundred years ago. This is really no improvement on the work of the Roman augurs.

BENARES*

> Let me make the superstitions of a nation and I care not who makes its laws or its songs either.
> —*Pudd'nhead Wilson's New Calendar*

Yes, the city of Benares is in effect just a big church, a religious hive, whose every cell is a temple, a shrine or a mosque, and whose every conceivable earthly and heavenly good is procurable under one roof, so to speak—a sort of Army and Navy Stores, theologically stocked.

I will make out a little itinerary for the pilgrim; then you will see how handy the system is, how convenient, how comprehensive. If you go to Benares with a serious desire to spiritually benefit yourself, you will find it valuable. I got some of the facts from conversations with the Rev. Mr. Parker and the others from his Guide to Benares; they are therefore trustworthy.

1. *Purification.* At sunrise you must go down to the Ganges and bathe, pray, and drink some of the water. This is for your general purification.

2. *Protection Against Hunger.* Next, you must fortify yourself against the sorrowful earthly ill just named. This you will do by worshiping for a moment in the Cow Temple. By the door of it you will find an image of Ganesh, son of

---

*Editor's title.

Shiva; it has the head of an elephant on a human body; its face and hands are of silver. You will worship it a little, and pass on, into a covered veranda, where you will find devotees reciting from the sacred books, with the help of instructors. In this place are groups of rude and dismal idols. You may contribute something for their support; then pass into the temple, a grim and stenchy place, for it is populous with sacred cows and with beggars. You will give something to the beggars, and "reverently kiss the tails" of such cows as pass along, for these cows are peculiarly holy, and this act of worship will secure you from hunger for the day.

3. *"The Poor Man's Friend."* You will next worship this god. He is at the bottom of a stone cistern in the temple of Dalbhyeswar, under the shade of a noble peepul tree on the bluff overlooking the Ganges, so you must go back to the river. The Poor Man's Friend is the god of *material prosperity* in general, and the god of the *rain* in particular. You will secure material prosperity, or both, by worshiping him. He is Shiva, under a new alias, and he abides in the bottom of that cistern, in the form of a stone lingam. You pour Ganges water over him, and in return for this homage you get the promised benefits. If there is any delay about the rain, you must pour water in until the cistern is full; the rain will then be sure to come.

4. *Fever.* At the Kedar Ghat you will find a long flight of stone steps leading down to the river. Half way down is a tank filled with sewage. Drink as much of it as you want. It is for fever.

5. *Smallpox.* Go straight from there to the central Ghat. At its upstream end you will find a small whitewashed building, which is a temple sacred to Sitala, goddess of smallpox. Her under-study is there—a rude human figure behind a brass screen. You will worship this for reasons to be furnished presently.

6. *The Well of Fate.* For certain reasons you will next go

and do homage at this well. You will find it in the Dandpan Temple, in the city. The sunlight falls into it from a square hole in the masonry above. You will approach it with awe, for your life is now at stake. You will bend over and look. If the fates are propitious, you will see your face pictured in the water far down in the well. If matters have been otherwise ordered, a sudden cloud will mask the sun and you will see nothing. This means that you have not six months to live. If you are already at the point of death, your circumstances are now serious. There is no time to lose. Let this world go, arrange for the next one. Handily situated, at your very elbow, is opportunity for this. You turn and worship the image of Maha Kal, the Great Fate, and happiness in the life to come is secured. If there is breath in your body yet, you should now make an effort to get a further lease of the present life. You have a chance. There is a chance for everything in this admirably stocked and wonderfully systemized Spiritual and Temporal Army and Navy Store. You must get yourself carried to the

7. *Well of Long Life.* This is within the precincts of the mouldering and venerable Briddhkal Temple, which is one of the oldest in Benares. You pass in by a stone image of the monkey god, Hanuman, and there, among the ruined courtyards, you will find a shallow pool of stagnant sewage. It smells like the best limburger cheese, and is filthy with the washings of rotting lepers, but that is nothing, bathe in it; bathe in it gratefully and worshipfully, for this is the Fountain of Youth; these are the Waters of Long Life. Your gray hairs will disappear, and with them your wrinkles and your rheumatism, the burdens of care and the weariness of age, and you will come out young, fresh, elastic, and full of eagerness for the new race of life. Now will come flooding upon you the manifold desires that haunt the dear dreams of the morning of life. You will go whither you will find

8. *Fulfillment of Desire.* To wit, to the Kameshwar Temple, sacred to Shiva as the Lord of Desires. Arrange for yours there. And if you like to look at idols among the pack and jam of temples, there you will find enough to stock a museum. You will begin to commit sins now with a fresh, new vivacity; therefore, it will be well to go frequently to a place where you can get

9. *Temporary Cleansing from Sin.* To wit, to the Well of the Earring. You must approach this with the profoundest reverence, for it is unutterably sacred. It is, indeed, the most sacred place in Benares, the very Holy of Holies, in the estimation of the people. It is a railed tank, with stone stairways leading down to the water. The water is not clean. Of course it could not be, for people are always bathing in it. As long as you choose to stand and look, you will see the files of sinners descending and ascending—descending soiled with sin, ascending purged from it. "The liar, the thief, the murderer, and the adulterer may here wash and be clean," says the Rev. Mr. Parker, in his book. Very well. I know Mr. Parker, and I believe it; but if anybody else had said it, I should consider him a person who had better go down in the tank and take another wash. The god Vishnu dug this tank. He had nothing to dig with but his "discus." I do not know what a discus is, but I know it is a poor thing to dig tanks with, because, by the time this one was finished, it was full of sweat—Vishnu's sweat. He constructed the site that Benares stands on, and afterward built the globe around it, and thought nothing of it, yet sweated like that over a little thing like this tank. One of these statements is doubtful. I do not know which one it is, but I think it difficult not to believe that a god who could build a world around Benares would not be intelligent enough to build it around the tank too, and not have to dig it. Youth, long life, temporary purification from sin, salvation through propiti-

ation of the Great Fate—these are all good. But you must do something more. You must

10. *Make Salvation Sure.* There are several ways. To get drowned in the Ganges is one, but that is not pleasant. To die within the limits of Benares is another; but that is a risky one, because you might be out of town when your time came. The best one of all is the Pilgrimage Around the City. You must walk; also, you must go barefoot. The tramp is forty-four miles, for the road winds out into the country a piece, and you will be marching five or six days. But you will have plenty of company. You will move with throngs and hosts of happy pilgrims whose radiant costumes will make the spectacle beautiful and whose glad songs and holy paeans of triumph will banish your fatigues and cheer your spirit; and at intervals there will be temples where you may sleep and be refreshed with food. The pilgrimage completed, you have purchased salvation, and paid for it. But you may not get it unless you

11. *Get Your Redemption Recorded.* You can get this done at the Sakhi Binayak Temple, and it is best to do it, for otherwise you might not be able to prove that you had made the pilgrimage in case the matter should some day come to be disputed. That temple is in a lane back of the Cow Temple. Over the door is a red image of Ganesh of the elephant head, son and heir of Shiva, and Prince of Wales to the Theological Monarchy, so to speak. Within is a god whose office it is to record your pilgrimage and be responsible for you. You will not see him, but you will see a Brahmin who will attend to the matter and take the money. If he should forget to collect the money, you can remind him. *He* knows that your salvation is now secure, but of course you would like to know it yourself. You have nothing to do but go and pray, and pay at the

12. *Well of the Knowledge of Salvation.* It is close to the

Golden Temple. There you will see, sculptured out of a single piece of black marble, a bull which is much larger than any living bull you have ever seen, and yet is not a good likeness after all. And there also you will see a very uncommon thing—an image of Shiva. You have seen his lingam fifty thousand times already, but this is Shiva himself, and said to be a good likeness. It has three eyes. He is the only god in the firm that has three. "The well is covered by a fine canopy of stone supported by forty pillars," and around it you will find what you have already seen at almost every shrine you have visited in Benares, a mob of devout and eager pilgrims. The sacred water is being ladled out to them; with it comes to them the knowledge, clear, thrilling, absolute, that they are saved; and you can see by their faces that there is one happiness in this world which is supreme, and to which no other joy is comparable. You receive your water, you make your deposit, and now what more would you have? Gold, diamonds, power, fame? All in a single moment these things have withered to dirt, dust, ashes. The world has nothing to give you now. For you it is bankrupt.

I do not claim that the pilgrims do their acts of worship in the order and sequence above charted out in this Itinerary of mine, but I think logic suggests that they ought to do so. Instead of a helter-skelter worship, we then have a definite starting-place, and a march which carries the pilgrim steadily forward by reasoned and logical progression to a definite goal. Thus, his Ganges bath in the early morning gives him an appetite; he kisses the cow-tails, and that removes it. It is now business hours, and longings for material prosperity rise in his mind, and he goes and pours water over Shiva's symbol; this insures the prosperity, but also brings on a rain, which gives him a fever. Then he drinks the sewage at the Kedar Ghat to cure the fever; it cures the fever but gives him the smallpox. He wishes to know how it is going to turn out; he goes to the Dandpan Temple and looks down the well. A clouded sun shows him that death is near. Logically his best course for the present, since he cannot tell at what moment he may die, is to secure a happy hereafter; this he does, through the agency of the Great Fate. He is safe, now, for heaven; his next move will naturally be to keep out of it as long as he can. Therefore he goes to the Briddhkal Temple and secures Youth and long life by bathing in a puddle of leper-pus which would kill a microbe. Logically, Youth has re-equipped him for sin and with the disposition to commit it; he will naturally go to the fane which is consecrated to the Fulfillment of Desires, and make arrangements. Logically, he will now go to the Well of the Earring from time to time to unload and freshen up for further banned enjoyments. But first and last and all the time he is human, and therefore in his reflective intervals he will always be speculating in "futures." He will make the Great Pilgrimage around the city and so make his salvation absolutely sure; he will also have record made of it, so that it may remain absolutely sure and not be forgotten or repudiated in the confusion of the Final Settlement. Logically, also, he will wish to have satisfying and tranquilizing *personal* knowledge that that salvation is secure; therefore he goes to the Well of the Knowledge of Salvation, adds that completing detail, and then goes about his affairs serene and content; serene and content, for he is now royally endowed with an advantage which no religion in this world could give him but his own; for henceforth he may commit as many million sins as he wants to and nothing can come of it.

Thus the system, properly and logically ordered, is neat,

compact, clearly defined, and covers the whole ground. I desire to recommend it to such as find the other systems too difficult, exacting, and irksome for the uses of this fretful brief life of ours.

However, let me not deceive any one. My Itinerary lacks a detail. I must put it in. The truth is, that after the pilgrim has faithfully followed the requirements of the Itinerary through to the end and has secured his salvation and also the personal knowledge of that fact, there is still an accident possible to him which can annul the whole thing. If he should ever cross to the other side of the Ganges and get caught out and die there he would at once come to life again in the form of an ass. Think of that, after all this trouble and expense. You see how capricious and uncertain salvation is there. The Hindoo has a childish and unreasoning aversion to being turned into an ass. It is hard to tell why. One could properly expect an ass to have an aversion to being turned into a Hindoo. One could understand that he could lose dignity by it; also self-respect, and nine-tenths of his intelligence. But the Hindoo changed into an ass wouldn't lose anything, unless you count his religion. And he would gain much—release from his slavery to two million gods and twenty million priests, fakeers, holy mendicants, and other sacred bacilli; he would escape the Hindoo hell; he would also escape the Hindoo heaven. These are advantages which the Hindoo ought to consider; then he would go over and die on the other side.

Benares is a religious Vesuvius. In its bowels the theological forces have been heaving and tossing, rumbling, thundering and quaking, boiling, and weltering and flaming and smoking for ages. But a little group of missionaries have taken post at its base, and they have hopes. There are the Baptist Missionary Society, the Church Missionary

Society, the London Missionary Society, the Wesleyan Missionary Society, and the Zenana Bible and Medical Mission. They have schools, and the principal work seems to be among the children. And no doubt that part of the work prospers best, for grown people everywhere are always likely to cling to the religion they were brought up in.

VI.

THE SOCIAL ORDER

The Bee

It was Maeterlinck who introduced me to the bee. I mean, in the psychical and in the poetical way. I had had a business introduction earlier. It was when I was a boy. It is strange that I should remember a formality like that so long; it must be nearly sixty years.

Bee scientists always speak of the bee as she. It is because all the important bees are of that sex. In the hive there is one married bee, called the queen; she has fifty thousand children; of these, about one hundred are sons; the rest are daughters. Some of the daughters are young maids, some are old maids, and are virgins and remain so.

Every spring the queen comes out of the hive and flies away with one of her sons and marries him. The honeymoon lasts only an hour or two; then the queen divorces her husband and returns home competent to lay two million eggs. This will be enough to last the year, but not more than enough, because hundreds of bees get drowned every day, and other hundreds are eaten by birds, and it is the queen's business to keep the population up to standard—say, fifty thousand. She must always have that many children on hand and efficient during the busy season, which is summer, or winter would catch the community short of food. She lays from two thousand to three thousand eggs a day, according to the demand; and she must exercise judgment, and not lay more than are needed in a slim flower-harvest, nor fewer than are required in a prodigal one, or the board of directors will dethrone her and elect a queen that has more sense.

There are always a few royal heirs in stock and ready to take her place—ready and more than anxious to do it, although she is their own mother. These girls are kept by themselves, and are regally fed and tended from birth. No other bees get such fine food as they get, or live such a high and luxurious life. By consequence they are larger and longer and sleeker than their working sisters. And they have a curved sting, shaped like a simitar, while the others have a straight one.

A common bee will sting any one or anybody, but a royalty stings royalties only. A common bee will sting and kill another common bee, for cause, but when it is necessary to kill the queen other ways are employed. When a queen has grown old and slack and does not lay eggs enough one of her royal daughters is allowed to come to attack her, the rest of the bees looking on at the duel and seeing fair play. It is a duel with the curved stings. If one of the fighters gets hard pressed and gives it up and runs, she is brought back and must try again—once, maybe twice; then, if she runs yet once more for her life, judicial death is her portion; her children pack themselves into a ball around her person and hold her in that compact grip two or three days, until she starves to death or is suffocated. Meantime the victor bee is receiving royal honors and performing the one royal function—laying eggs.

As regards the ethics of the judicial assassination of the queen, that is a matter of politics, and will be discussed later, in its proper place.

During substantially the whole of her short life of five or six years the queen lives in the Egyptian darkness and

The Bee

stately seclusion of the royal apartments, with none about her but plebeian servants, who give her empty lip-affection in place of the love which her heart hungers for; who spy upon her in the interest of her waiting heirs, and report and exaggerate her defects and deficiencies to them; who fawn upon her and flatter her to her face and slander her behind her back; who grovel before her in the day of her power and forsake her in her age and weakness. There she sits, friendless, upon her throne through the long night of her life, cut off from the consoling sympathies and sweet companionship and loving endearments which she craves, by the gilded barriers of her awful rank; a forlorn exile in her own house and home, weary object of formal ceremonies and machine-made worship, winged child of the sun, native to the free air and the blue skies and the flowery fields, doomed by the splendid accident of her birth to trade this priceless heritage for a black captivity, a tinsel grandeur, and a loveless life, with shame and insult at the end and a cruel death—and condemned by the human instinct in her to hold the bargain valuable!

Huber, Lubbock, Maeterlinck—in fact, all the great authorities—are agreed in denying that the bee is a member of the human family. I do not know why they have done this, but I think it is from dishonest motives. Why, the innumerable facts brought to light by their own painstaking and exhaustive experiments prove that if there is a master fool in the world, it is the bee. That seems to settle it.

But that is the way of the scientist. He will spend thirty years in building up a mountain range of facts with the intent to prove a certain theory; then he is so happy in his achievement that as a rule he overlooks the main chief fact of all—that his accumulation proves an entirely different thing. When you point out this miscarriage to him he does not answer your letters; when you call to convince him, the servant prevaricates and you do not get in. Scientists have odious manners, except when you prop up their theory; then you can borrow money of them.

To be strictly fair, I will concede that now and then one of them will answer your letter, but when they do they avoid the issue—you cannot pin them down. When I discovered that the bee was human I wrote about it to all those scientists whom I have just mentioned. For evasions, I have seen nothing to equal the answers I got.

After the queen, the personage next in importance in the hive is the virgin. The virgins are fifty thousand or one hundred thousand in number, and they are the workers, the laborers. No work is done, in the hive or out of it, save by them. The males do not work, the queen does no work, unless laying eggs is work, but it does not seem so to me. There are only two million of them, anyway, and all of five months to finish the contract in. The distribution of work in a hive is as cleverly and elaborately specialized as it is in a vast American machine-shop or factory. A bee that has been trained to one of the many and various industries of the concern doesn't know how to exercise any other, and would be offended if asked to take a hand in anything outside of her profession. She is as human as a cook; and if you should ask the cook to wait on the table, you know what will happen. Cooks will play the piano if you like, but they draw the line there. In my time I have asked a cook to chop wood, and I know about these things. Even the hired girl has her frontiers; true, they are vague, they are ill-defined, even flexible, but they are there. This is not conjecture; it is founded on the absolute. And then the butler. You ask the butler to wash the dog. It is just as I say; there is much to be learned in these ways, without going to books. Books are very well, but books do not cover the whole domain of esthetic human culture. Pride of profession is one of the boniest bones in existence, if not the boniest. Without doubt it is so in the hive.

A Curious Scrap of History

Marion City, on the Mississippi River, in the State of Missouri—a village; time, 1845. La Bourboule-les-Bains, France—a village; time, the end of June, 1894. I was in the one village in that early time; I am in the other now. These times and places are sufficiently wide apart, yet today I have the strange sense of being thrust back into that Missourian village and of reliving certain stirring days that I lived there so long ago.

Last Saturday night the life of the President of the French Republic was taken by an Italian assassin. Last night a mob surrounded our hotel, shouting, howling, singing the "Marseillaise," and pelting our windows with sticks and stones; for we have Italian waiters, and the mob demanded that they be turned out of the house instantly—to be drubbed, and then driven out of the village. Everybody in the hotel remained up until far into the night, and experienced the several kinds of terror which one reads about in books which tell of night attacks by Italians and by French mobs: the growing roar of the oncoming crowd; the arrival, with rain of stones and a crash of glass; the withdrawal to rearrange plans—followed by a silence ominous, threatening, and harder to bear than even the active siege and the noise. The landlord and the two village policemen stood their ground, and at last the mob was persuaded to go away and leave our Italians in peace. Today four of the ringleaders have been sentenced to heavy punishment of a public sort—and are become local heroes, by consequence.

That is the very mistake which was at first made in the Missourian village half a century ago. The mistake was repeated and repeated—just as France is doing in these later months.

In our village we had our Ravochals, our Henrys, our Vaillants; and in a humble way our Cesario—I hope I have spelled this name wrong. Fifty years ago we passed through, in all essentials, what France has been passing through during the past two or three years, in the matter of periodical frights, horrors, and shudderings.

In several details the parallels are quaintly exact. In that day, for a man to speak out openly and proclaim himself an enemy of negro slavery was simply to proclaim himself a madman. For he was blaspheming against the holiest thing known to a Missourian, and could *not* be in his right mind. For a man to proclaim himself an anarchist in France, three years ago, was to proclaim himself a madman—he could not be in his right mind.

Now the original first blasphemer against any institution profoundly venerated by a community is quite sure to be in earnest; his followers and imitators may be humbugs and self-seekers, but he himself is sincere—his heart is in his protest.

Robert Hardy was our first *abolitionist*—awful name! He was a journeyman cooper, and worked in the big cooper-shop belonging to the great pork-packing establishment which was Marion City's chief pride and sole source of prosperity. He was a New-Englander, a stranger. And, being a stranger, he was of course regarded as an inferior person—for that has been human nature from Adam down—and of course, also, he was made to feel unwelcome, for this is the ancient law with man and the other animals. Hardy was thirty years old, and a bachelor; pale, given to reverie and reading. He was reserved, and seemed to prefer the isolation which had fallen to his lot. He was treated to many side remarks by his fellows, but as he did not resent them it was decided that he was a coward.

All of a sudden he proclaimed himself an abolitionist—straight out and publicly! He said that negro slavery was a crime, an infamy. For a moment the town was paralyzed with astonishment; then it broke into a fury of rage and swarmed toward the cooper-shop to lynch Hardy. But the Methodist minister made a powerful speech to them and stayed their hands. He proved to them that Hardy was insane and not responsible for his words; that no man *could* be sane and utter such words.

So Hardy was saved. Being insane, he was allowed to go on talking. He was found to be good entertainment. Several nights running he made abolition speeches in the open air, and all the town flocked to hear and laugh. He implored them to believe him sane and sincere, and have pity on the poor slaves, and take measurements for the restoration of their stolen rights, or in no long time blood would flow—blood, blood, rivers of blood!

It was great fun. But all of a sudden the aspect of things changed. A slave came flying from Palmyra, the county-seat, a few miles back, and was about to escape in a canoe to Illinois and freedom in the dull twilight of the approaching dawn, when the town constable seized him. Hardy happened along and tried to rescue the negro; there was a struggle, and the constable did not come out of it alive. Hardy crossed the river with the negro, and then came back to give himself up. All this took time, for the Mississippi is not a French brook, like the Seine, the Loire, and those other rivulets, but is a real river nearly a mile wide. The town was on hand in force by now, but the Methodist preacher and the sheriff had already made arrangements in the interest of order; so Hardy was surrounded by a strong guard and safely conveyed to the village calaboose in spite of all the effort of the mob to get hold of him. The reader will have begun to perceive that this Methodist minister was a prompt man; a prompt man, with active hands and a good headpiece. Williams was his name—Damon Williams; Damon Williams in public, Damnation Williams in private, because he was so powerful on that theme and so frequent.

The excitement was prodigious. The constable was the first man who had ever been killed in the town. The event was by long odds the most imposing in the town's history. It lifted the humble village into sudden importance; its name was in everybody's mouth for twenty miles around. And so was the name of Robert Hardy—Robert Hardy, the stranger, the despised. In a day he was become the person of most consequence in the region, the only person talked about. As to those other coopers, they found their position curiously changed—they were important people, or unimportant, now, in proportion as to how large or how small had been their intercourse with the new celebrity. The two or three who had really been on a sort of familiar footing with him found themselves objects of admiring interest with the public and of envy with their shopmates.

The village weekly journal had lately gone into new hands. The new man was an enterprising fellow, and he made the most of the tragedy. He issued an extra. Then he put up posters promising to devote his whole paper to matters connected with the great event—there would be a full and intensely interesting biography of the murderer, and even a portrait of him. He was as good as his word. He carved the portrait himself, on the back of a wooden type—and a terror it was to look at. It made a great commotion, for this was the first time the village paper had ever contained a picture. The village was very proud. The output of the paper was ten times as great as it had ever been before, yet every copy was sold.

When the trial came on, people came from all the farms around, and from Hannibal, and Quincy, and even from Keokuk; and the court-house could hold only a fraction of the crowd that applied for admission. The trial was published in the village paper, with fresh and still more trying pictures of the accused.

Hardy was convicted, and hanged—a mistake. People came from miles around to see the hanging; they brought cakes and cider, also the women and children, and made a picnic of the matter. It was the largest crowd the village had ever seen. The rope that hanged Hardy was eagerly bought up, in inch samples, for everybody wanted a memento of the memorable event.

Martyrdom gilded with notoriety has its fascinations. Within one week afterward four young lightweights in the village proclaimed themselves abolitionists! In life Hardy had not been able to make a convert; everybody laughed at him; but nobody could laugh at his legacy. The four swaggered around with their slouch-hats pulled down over their faces, and hinted darkly at awful possibilities. The people were troubled and afraid, and showed it. And they were stunned, too; they could not understand it. "Abolitionist" had always been a term of shame and horror; yet here were four young men who were not only not ashamed to bear that name, but were grimly proud of it. Respectable young men they were, too—of good families, and brought up in the church. Ed Smith, the printer's apprentice, nineteen, had been the head Sunday-school boy, and had once recited three thousand Bible verses without making a break. Dick Savage, twenty, the baker's apprentice; Will Joyce, twenty-two, journeyman blacksmith; and Henry Taylor, twenty-four, tobacco-stemmer—were the other three. They were all of a sentimental cast; they were all romance-readers; they all wrote poetry, such as it was; they were all vain and foolish; but they had never before been suspected of having anything bad in them.

They withdrew from society, and grew more and more mysterious and dreadful. They presently achieved the distinction of being denounced by names from the pulpit—which made an immense stir! This was grandeur, this was fame. They were envied by all the other young fellows now. This was natural. Their company grew—grew alarmingly. They took a name. It was a secret name, and was divulged to no outsider; publicly they were simply the abolitionists. They had pass-words, grips, and signs; they had secret meetings; their initiations were conducted with gloomy pomps and ceremonies, at midnight.

They always spoke of Hardy as "the Martyr," and every little while they moved through the principal street in procession—at midnight, black-robed, masked, to the measured tap of the solemn drum—on pilgrimage to the Martyr's grave, where they went through with some majestic fooleries and swore vengeance upon his murderers. They gave previous notice of the pilgrimage by small posters, and warned everybody to keep indoors and darken all houses along the route, and leave the road empty. These warnings were obeyed, for there was a skull and crossbones at the top of the poster.

When this kind of thing had been going on about eight weeks, a quite natural thing happened. A few men of character and grit woke up out of the nightmare of fear which had been stupefying their faculties, and began to discharge scorn and scoffings at themselves and the community for enduring this child's-play; and at the same time they proposed to end it straightway. Everybody felt an uplift; life was breathed into their dead spirits; their courage rose and they began to feel like men again. This was on a Saturday. All day the new feeling grew and strengthened; it grew with a rush; it brought inspiration and cheer with it. Midnight saw a united community, full of zeal and pluck, and with a clearly defined and welcome piece of work in front of it. The best organizer and strongest and bitterest talker on that great Saturday was the Presbyterian clergyman who had denounced the original four from his pulpit—Rev. Hiram Fletcher—and he promised to use his pulpit in the public interest again now. On the morrow he had revelations to make, he said—secrets of the dreadful society.

But the revelations were never made. At half past two in the morning the dead silence of the village was broken by a crashing explosion, and the town patrol saw the preacher's house spring in a wreck of whirling fragments into the sky. The preacher was killed, together with a negro woman, his only slave and servant.

The town was paralyzed again, and with reason. To struggle against a visible enemy is a thing worth while, and there is a plenty of men who stand always ready to undertake it; but to struggle against an invisible one—an invisible one who sneaks in and does his awful work in the dark and leaves no trace—that is another matter. That is a thing to make the bravest tremble and hold back.

The cowed populace were afraid to go to the funeral. The man who was to have had a packed church to hear him expose and denounce the common enemy had but a handful to see him buried. The coroner's jury had brought in a verdict of "death by the visitation of God," for no witness came forward; if any existed they prudently kept out of the way. Nobody seemed sorry. Nobody wanted to see the terrible secret society provoked into the commission of further outrages. Everybody wanted the tragedy hushed up, ignored, forgotten, if possible.

And so there was a bitter surprise and an unwelcome one when Will Joyce, the blacksmith's journeyman, came out and proclaimed himself the assassin! Plainly he was not minded to be robbed of his glory. He made his proclamation, and stuck to it. Stuck to it, and insisted upon a trial. Here was an ominous thing; here was a new and peculiarly formidable terror, for a motive was revealed here which society could not hope to deal with successfully—*vanity*, thirst for notoriety. If men were going to kill for notoriety's sake, and to win the glory of newspaper renown, a big trial, and a showy execution, what possible invention of man could discourage or deter them? The town was in a sort of panic; it did not know what to do.

However, the grand jury had to take hold of the matter—it had no choice. It brought in a true bill, and presently the case went to the county court. The trial was a fine sensation. The prisoner was the principal witness for the prosecution. He gave a full account of the assassination; he furnished even the minutest particulars: how he deposited his keg of powder and laid his train—from the house to such-and-such a spot; how George Ronalds and Henry Hart came along just then, smoking, and he borrowed Hart's cigar and fired the train with it, shouting, "Down with all slave-tyrants!" and how Hart and Ronalds made no effort to capture him, but ran away, and had never come forward to testify yet.

But they had to testify now, and they did—and pitiful it was to see how reluctant they were, and how scared. The crowded house listened to Joyce's fearful tale with a profound and breathless interest, and in a deep hush which was not broken till he broke it himself, in concluding, with a roaring repetition of his "Death to all slave-tyrants!"—

which came so unexpectedly and so startlingly that it made everyone present catch his breath and gasp.

The trial was put in the paper, with biography and large portrait, with other slanderous and insane pictures, and the edition sold beyond imagination.

The execution of Joyce was a fine and picturesque thing. It drew a vast crowd. Good places in trees and seats on rail fences sold for half a dollar apiece; lemonade and gingerbread-stands had great prosperity. Joyce recited a furious and fantastic and denunciatory speech on the scaffold which had imposing passages of school-boy eloquence in it, and gave him a reputation on the spot as an orator, and his name, later, in the society's records, of the "Martyr Orator." He went to his death breathing slaughter and charging his society to "avenge his murder." If he knew anything of human nature he knew that to plenty of young fellows present in that great crowd he was a grand hero—and enviably situated.

He was hanged. It was a mistake. Within a month from his death the society which he had honored had twenty new members, some of them earnest, determined men. They did not court distinction in the same way, but they celebrated his martyrdom. The crime which had been obscure and despised had become lofty and glorified.

Such things were happening all over the country. Wild-brained martyrdom was succeeded by uprising and organization. Then, in natural order, followed riot, insurrection, and the wrack and restitutions of war. It was bound to come, and it would naturally come in that way. It has been the manner of reform since the beginning of the world.

VII.

LITERATURE AND ART

How to Tell a Story

I do not claim that I can tell a story as it ought to be told. I only claim to know how a story ought to be told, for I have been almost daily in the company of the most expert storytellers for many years.

There are several kinds of stories, but only one difficult kind—the humorous. I will talk mainly about that one. The humorous story is American, the comic story is English, the witty story is French. The humorous story depends for its effect upon the *manner* of the telling; the comic story and the witty story upon the *matter*.

The humorous story may be spun out to great length, and may wander around as much as it pleases, and arrive nowhere in particular; but the comic and witty stories must be brief and end with a point. The humorous story bubbles gently along, the others burst.

The humorous story is strictly a work of art—high and delicate art—and only an artist can tell it; but no art is necessary in telling the comic and the witty story; anybody can do it. The art of telling a humorous story—understand, I mean by word of mouth, not print—was created in America, and has remained at home.

The humorous story is told gravely; the teller does his best to conceal the fact that he even dimly suspects that there is anything funny about it; but the teller of the comic story tells you beforehand that it is one of the funniest things he has ever heard, then tells it with eager delight, and is the first person to laugh when he gets through. And sometimes, if he has had good success, he is so glad and happy that he will repeat the "nub" of it and glance around from face to face, collecting applause, and then repeat it again. It is a pathetic thing to see.

Very often, of course, the rambling and disjointed humorous story finishes with a nub, point, snapper, or whatever you like to call it. Then the listener must be alert, for in many cases the teller will divert attention from that nub by dropping it in a carefully casual and indifferent way, with the pretense that he does not know it is a nub.

Artemus Ward used that trick a good deal; then when the belated audience presently caught the joke he would look up with innocent surprise, as if wondering what they had found to laugh at. Dan Setchell used it before him, Nye and Riley and others use it to-day.

But the teller of the comic story does not slur the nub; he shouts it at you—every time. And when he prints it, in England, France, Germany, and Italy, he italicizes it, puts some whopping exclamation-points after it, and sometimes explains it in a parenthesis. All of which is very depressing, and makes one want to renounce joking and lead a better life.

Let me set down an instance of the comic method, using an anecdote which has been popular all over the world for twelve or fifteen hundred years. The teller tells it in this way:

The Wounded Soldier

In the course of a certain battle a soldier whose leg had been shot off appealed to another soldier who was hurrying by to carry him to the rear, informing him at the same time of the loss which he had sustained;

whereupon the generous son of Mars, shouldering the unfortunate, proceeded to carry out his desire. The bullets and cannon-balls were flying in all directions, and presently one of the latter took the wounded man's head off—without, however, his deliverer being aware of it. In no long time he was hailed by an officer, who said:

"Where are you going with that carcass?"

"To the rear, sir—he's lost his leg!"

"His leg, forsooth?" responded the astonished officer; "you mean his head, you booby."

Whereupon the soldier dispossessed himself of his burden, and stood looking down upon it in great perplexity. At length he said:

"It is true, sir, just as you have said." Then after a pause he added, "*But he* TOLD *me* IT WAS HIS LEG!!!!!"

Here the narrator bursts into explosion after explosion of thunderous horse-laughter, repeating that nub from time to time through his gasping and shriekings and suffocatings.

It takes only a minute and a half to tell that in its comic-story form; and isn't worth the telling, after all. Put into the humorous-story form it takes ten minutes, and is about the funniest thing I have ever listened to—as James Whitcomb Riley tells it.

He tells it in the character of a dull-witted old farmer who has just heard it for the first time, thinks it is unspeakably funny, and is trying to repeat it to a neighbor. But he can't remember it; so he gets all mixed up and wanders helplessly round and round, putting in tedious details that don't belong in the tale and only retard it; taking them out conscientiously and putting in others that are just as useless; making minor mistakes now and then and stopping to correct them and explain how he came to make them; remembering things which he forgot to put in their proper place and going back to put them in there; stopping his narrative a good while in order to try to recall the name of the soldier that was hurt, and finally remembering that the soldier's name was not mentioned, and remarking placidly that the name is of no real importance, anyway—better, of course, if one knew it, but not essential, after all—and so on, and so on, and so on.

The teller is innocent and happy and pleased with himself, and has to stop every little while to hold himself in and keep from laughing outright; and does hold in, but his body quakes in a jelly-like way with interior chuckles; and at the end of the ten minutes the audience have laughed until they are exhausted, and the tears are running down their faces.

The simplicity and innocence and sincerity and unconsciousness of the old farmer are perfectly simulated, and the result is a performance which is thoroughly charming and delicious. This is art—and fine and beautiful, and only a master can compass it; but a machine could tell the other story.

To string incongruities and absurdities together in a wandering and sometimes purposeless way, and seem innocently unaware that they are absurdities, is the basis of the American art, if my position is correct. Another feature is the slurring of the point. A third is the dropping of a studied remark apparently without knowing it, as if one were thinking aloud. The fourth and last is the pause.

Artemus Ward dealt in numbers three and four a good deal. He would begin to tell with great animation something which he seemed to think was wonderful; then lose confidence, and after an apparently absent-minded pause add an incongruous remark in a soliloquizing way; and that was the remark intended to explode the mine—and it did.

For instance, he would say eagerly, excitedly, "I once knew a man in New Zealand who hadn't a tooth in his head"—here his animation would die out; a silent, reflective pause would follow, then he would say dreamily, and as if to himself, "and yet that man could beat a drum better than any man I ever saw."

The pause is an exceedingly important feature in any kind of story, and a frequently recurring feature, too. It is a dainty thing, and delicate, and also uncertain and treacherous; for it must be exactly the right length—no more and no less—or it fails of its purpose and makes trouble. If the pause is too short the impressive point is passed, and the audience have had time to divine that a surprise is intended—and then you can't surprise them, of course.

On the platform I used to tell a negro ghost story that had a pause in front of the snapper on the end, and that pause was the most important thing in the whole story. If I got it the right length precisely, I could spring the finishing ejaculation with effect enough to make some impressible girl deliver a startled little yelp and jump out of her seat—and that was what I was after. This story was called "The Golden Arm," and was told in this fashion. You can practise with it yourself—and mind you look out for the pause and get it right.

The Golden Arm

Once 'pon a time dey wuz a monsus mean man, en he live 'way out in de prairie all 'lone by hisself, 'cep'n he had a wife. En bimeby she died, en he tuck en toted her way out dah in de prairie en buried her. Well, she had a golden arm—all solid gold, fum de shoulder down. He wuz pow'ful mean—pow'ful; en dat night he couldn't sleep, caze he want dat golden arm so bad.

When it come midnight he couldn't stan' it no mo'; so he git up, he did, en tuck his lantern en shoved out thoo de storm en dug her up en got de golden arm; en he bent his head down 'gin de win', en plowed en plowed en plowed thoo de snow. Den all on a sudden he stop (make a considerable pause here, and look startled, and take a listening attitude) en say: "My *lan'*, what's dat?"

En he listen—en listen—en de win' say (set your teeth together and imitate the wailing and wheezing singsong of the wind), "Bzzz-z-zzz"—en den, way back yonder whah de grave is, he hear a *voice!*—he hear a voice all mix' up in de win'—can't hardly tell 'em 'part—"Bzzz-zzz—W-h-o—g-o-t—m-y—g-o-l-d-e-n—*arm?*"(You must begin to shiver violently now.)

En he begin to shiver en shake, en say, "Oh, my! *Oh, my lan'!*" en de win' blow de lantern out, en de snow en sleet blow in his face en mos' choke him, en he start a-plowin' knee-deep towards home mos' dead, he so sk'yerd—en pooty soon he hear de voice agin, en (pause) it 'us comin' *after* him! "Bzzz—zzz—zzz—W-h-o—g-o-t—m-y—g-o-l-d-e-n—*arm?*"

When he git to de pasture he hear it agin—closter now, en a-*comin'!* —a-comin' back dah in de dark en de storm—(repeat the wind and the voice). When he git to de house he rush up-stairs en jump in de bed en kiver up, head and years, en lay dah shiverin' en shakin'—en den way out dah he hear it *agin!*—en a-*comin'!* En bimeby he hear (pause—awed, listening attitude)—pat—pat—pat—*hit's a-comin' upstairs!* Den he hear de latch, en he know it's in de room!

Den pooty soon he know it's a-*stannin' by de bed!* (Pause.) Den—he know it's a-*bendin' down over him*—en he cain't skasely git his breath! Den—den—he seem to feel someth'n *c-o-l-d,* right down 'most agin his head! (Pause.)

Den de voice say, *right at his year*—"W-h-o—g-o-t—m-y—g-o-l-d-e-n *arm?*" (You must wail it out very plaintively and accusingly; then you stare steadily and impressively into the face of the farthest-gone auditor,—a girl, preferably,—and let that awe-inspiring pause begin to build itself in the deep hush. When it has reached exactly the right length, jump suddenly at that girl and yell, *"You've* got it!"

If you've got the *pause* right, she'll fetch a dear little yelp and spring right out of her shoes. But you *must* get the pause right; and you will find it the most troublesome and aggravating and uncertain thing you ever undertook.

Disappearance of Literature

It wasn't necessary for your chairman to apologize for me in Germany. It wasn't necessary at all. Instead of that he ought to have impressed upon those poor benighted Teutons the service I rendered them. Their language had needed untangling for a good many years. Nobody else seemed to want to take the job, and so I took it, and I flatter myself that I made a pretty good job of it. The Germans have an inhuman way of cutting up their verbs. Now a verb has a hard time enough of it in this world when it's all together. It's downright inhuman to split it up. But that's just what those Germans do. They take part of a verb and put it down here, like a stake, and they take the other part of it and put it away over yonder like another stake, and between these two limits they just shovel in German. I maintain that there is no necessity for apologizing for a man who helped in a small way to stop such mutilation.

We have heard a discussion tonight on the disappearance of literature. That's no new thing. That's what certain kinds of literature have been doing for several years. The fact is, my friends, that the fashion in literature changes, and the literary tailors have to change their cuts or go out of business. Professor Winchester here, if I remember fairly correctly what he said, remarked that few, if any, of the novels produced to-day would live as long as the novels of Walter Scott. That may be his notion. Maybe he is right; but so far as I am concerned, I don't care if they don't.

Professor Winchester also said something about there being no modern epics like *Paradise Lost*. I guess he's right. He talked as if he was pretty familiar with that piece of literary work, and nobody would suppose that he never had read it. I don't believe any of you have ever read *Paradise Lost*, and you don't want to. That's something that you just want to take on trust. It's a classic, just as Professor Winchester says, and it meets his definition of a classic—something that everybody wants to have read and nobody wants to read.

Professor Trent also had a good deal to say about the disappearance of literature. He said that Scott would outlive all his critics. I guess that's true. The fact of the business is, you've got to be one of two ages to appreciate Scott. When you're eighteen you can read *Ivanhoe*, and you want to wait until you are ninety to read some of the rest. It takes a pretty well-regulated, abstemious critic to live ninety years.

But as much as these two gentlemen have talked about the disappearance of literature, they didn't say anything about my books. Maybe they think they've disappeared. If they do, that just shows their ignorance on the general subject of literature. I am not as young as I was several years ago, and maybe I'm not so fashionable, but I'd be willing to take my chances with Mr. Scott tomorrow morning in selling a piece of literature to the Century Publishing Company. And I haven't got much of a pull here, either. I often think that the highest compliment ever paid to my poor efforts was paid by Darwin through President Eliot, of Harvard College. At least, Eliot said it was a compliment, and I always take the opinion of great men like college presidents on all such subjects as that.

I went out to Cambridge one day a few years ago and called on President Eliot. In the course of the conversation he said that he had just returned from England, and that he was very much touched by what he considered the high compliment Darwin was paying to my books, and he went on to tell me something like this:

"Do you know that there is one room in Darwin's house, his bedroom, where the housemaid is never allowed to touch two things? One is a plant he is growing and studying while it grows" (it was one of those insect-devouring plants which consumed bugs and beetles and things for the particular delectation of Mr. Darwin) "and the other some books that lie on the night table at the head of his bed. They are your books, Mr. Clemens, and Mr. Darwin reads them every night to lull him to sleep."

My friends, I thoroughly appreciated that compliment, and considered it the highest one that was ever paid to me. To be the means of soothing to sleep a brain teeming with bugs and squirming things like Darwin's was something that I had never hoped for, and now that he is dead I never hope to be able to do it again.

The License of Art*

I wonder why some things are? For instance, Art is allowed as much indecent license to-day as in earlier times—but the privileges of Literature in this respect have been sharply curtailed within the past eighty or ninety years. Fielding and Smollett could portray the beastliness of their day in the beastliest language; we have plenty of foul subjects to deal with in our day, but we are not allowed to approach them very near, even with nice and guarded forms of speech. But not so with Art. The brush may still deal freely with any subject, however revolting or indelicate. It makes a body ooze sarcasm at every pore, to go about Rome and Florence and see what this last generation has been doing with the statues. These works, which had stood in innocent nakedness for ages, are all fig-leaved now. Yes, every one of them. Nobody noticed their nakedness before, perhaps; nobody can help noticing it now, the fig-leaf makes it so conspicuous. But the comical thing about it all, is, that the fig-leaf is confined to cold and pallid marble, which would be still cold and unsuggestive without this sham and ostentatious symbol of modesty, whereas warm-blooded paintings which do really need it have in no case been furnished with it.

At the door of the Ufizzi, in Florence, one is confronted by statues of a man and a woman, noseless, battered, black

*Editor's title.

with accumulated grime,—they hardly suggest human beings—yet these ridiculous creatures have been thoughtfully and conscientiously fig-leaved by this fastidious generation. You enter, and proceed to that most-visited little gallery that exists in the world—the Tribune—and there, against the wall, without obstructing rag or leaf, you may look your fill upon the foulest, the vilest, the obscenest picture the world possesses—Titian's Venus. It isn't that she is naked and stretched out on a bed—no, it is the attitude of one of her arms and hand. If I ventured to describe that attitude, there would be a fine howl—but there the Venus lies, for anybody to gloat over that wants to—and there she has a right to lie, for she is a work of art, and Art has its privileges. I saw young girls stealing furtive glances at her; I saw young men gaze long and absorbedly at her; I saw aged, infirm men hang upon her charms with a pathetic interest. How I should like to describe her—just to see what a holy indignation I could stir up in the world—just to hear the unreflecting average man deliver himself about my grossness and coarseness, and all that. The world says that no worded description of a moving spectacle is a hundredth part as moving as the same spectacle seen with one's own eyes—yet the world is willing to let its son and its daughter and itself look at Titian's beast, but won't stand a description of it in words. Which shows that the world is not as consistent as it might be.

There are pictures of nude women which suggest no impure thought—I am well aware of that. I am not railing at such. What I am trying to emphasize is the fact that Titian's Venus is very far from being one of that sort. Without any question it was painted for a bagnio and it was probably refused because it was a trifle too strong. In truth, it is too strong for any place but a public Art Gallery. Titian has two

Venuses in the Tribune; persons who have seen them will easily remember which one I am referring to.

In every gallery in Europe there are hideous pictures of blood, carnage, oozing brains, putrefaction—pictures portraying intolerable suffering—pictures alive with every conceivable horror, wrought out in dreadful detail—and similar pictures are being put on the canvas every day and publicly exhibited—without a growl from anybody—for they are innocent, they are inoffensive, being works of art. But suppose a literary artist ventured to go into a pain-staking and elaborate description of one of these grisly things—the critics would skin him alive. Well, let it go, it cannot be helped; Art retains her privileges, Literature has lost hers. Somebody else may cipher out the whys and the wherefores and the consistencies of it—I haven't got time.

Titian's Venus defiles and disgraces the Tribune, there is no softening that fact, but his "Moses" glorifies it. The simple truthfulness of this noble work wins the heart and the applause of every visitor, be he learned or ignorant. After wearying oneself with the acres of stuffy, sappy, expressionless babies that populate the canvases of the Old Masters of Italy, it is refreshing to stand before this peerless child and feel that thrill which tells you you are at last in the presence of the real thing. This is a human child, this is genuine. You have seen him a thousand times—you have seen him just as he is here—and you confess, without reserve, that Titian *was* a Master. The doll-faces of other painted babes may mean one thing, they may mean another, but with the "Moses" the case is different. The most famous of all the art critics has said, "There is no room for doubt, here—plainly this child is in trouble."

I consider that the "Moses" has no equal among the works of the Old Masters, except it be the divine Hair Trunk of Bassano. I feel sure that if all the other Old Masters were lost and only these two preserved, the world would be the gainer by it.

My sole purpose in going to Florence was to see this immortal "Moses," and by good fortune I was just in time, for they were already preparing to remove it to a more private and better protected place because a fashion of robbing the great galleries was prevailing in Europe at the time.

I got a capable artist to copy the picture; Pannemaker, the engraver of Doré's books, engraved it for me, and I have the pleasure of laying it before the reader in this volume.

We took a turn to Rome and some other Italian cities—then to Munich, and thence to Paris—partly for exercise, but mainly because these things were in our projected program, and it was only right that we should be faithful to it.

From Paris I branched out and walked through Holland and Belgium, procuring an occasional lift by rail or canal when tired, and I had a tolerably good time of it "by and large." I worked Spain and other regions through agents to save time and shoe leather.

We crossed to England, and then made the homeward passage in the Cunarder, *Gallia,* a very fine ship. I was glad to get home—immeasurably glad; so glad, in fact, that it did not seem possible that anything could ever get me out of the country again. I had not enjoyed a pleasure abroad which seemed to me to compare with the pleasure I felt in seeing New York harbor again. Europe has many advantages which we have not, but they do not compensate for a good many still more valuable ones which exist nowhere but in our own country. Then we are such a homeless lot when we are over there! So are Europeans themselves, for that matter. They live in dark and chilly vast tombs—costly enough, may be, but without conveniences. To be condemned to live as the average European family lives would make life a pretty heavy burden to the average American family.

On the whole, I think that short visits to Europe are better for us than long ones. The former preserve us from becoming Europeanized; they keep our pride of country intact, and at the same time they intensify our affection for our country and our people; whereas long visits have the effect of dulling those feelings,—at least in the majority of cases. I think that one who mixes much with Americans long resident abroad must arrive at this conclusion.

VIII.

THE WORLD AT LARGE

IMPERIAL HONORS TO AN AMERICAN

An acquaintance of mine said the other day that he was doubtless the only American visitor to the Exposition who had had the high honor of being escorted by the Emperor's bodyguard. I said with unobtrusive frankness that I was astonished that such a long-legged, lantern-jawed, unprepossessing-looking specter as he should be singled out for a distinction like that, and asked how it came about. He said he had attended a great military review in the Champ de Mars some time ago, and while the multitude about him was growing thicker and thicker every moment he observed an open space inside the railing. He left his carriage and went into it. He was the only person there, and so he had plenty of room, and the situation being central, he could see all the preparations going on about the field. By and by there was a sound of music, and soon the Emperor of the French and the Emperor of Austria, escorted by the famous *Cent Gardes,* entered the enclosure. They seemed not to observe him, but directly, in response to a sign from the commander of the guard, a young lieutenant came toward him with a file of his men following, halted, raised his hand, and gave the military salute, and then said in a low voice that he was sorry to have to disturb a stranger and a gentleman, but the place was sacred to royalty. Then this New Jersey phantom rose up and bowed and begged pardon, then with the officer beside him, the file of men marching behind him, and with every mark of respect, he was escorted to his carriage by the imperial *Cent Gardes!* The officer saluted again and fell back, the New Jersey sprite bowed in return and had presence of mind enough to pretend that he had simply called on a matter of private business with those emperors, and so waved them an adieu and drove from the field!

Imagine a poor Frenchman ignorantly intruding upon a public rostrum sacred to some sixpenny dignitary in America. The police would scare him to death first with a storm of their elegant blasphemy, and then pull him to pieces getting him away from there. We are measurably superior to the French in some things, but they are immeasurably our betters in others.

Snobs, at Home and Abroad

We have been pretty much everywhere in our gondola. We have bought beads and photographs in the stores and wax matches in the Great Square of St. Mark. The last remark suggests a digression. Everybody goes to this vast square in the evening. The military bands play in the center of it and countless couples of ladies and gentlemen promenade up and down on either side, and platoons of them are constantly drifting away toward the old cathedral, and by the venerable column with the Winged Lion of St. Mark on its top, and out to where the boats lie moored; and other platoons are as constantly arriving from the gondolas and joining the great throng. Between the promenaders and the sidewalks are seated hundreds and hundreds of people at small tables, smoking and taking *granita* (a first cousin to ice cream); on the sidewalks are more employing themselves in the same way. The shops in the first floor of the tall rows of buildings that wall in three sides of the square are brilliantly lighted, the air is filled with music and merry voices, and altogether the scene is as bright and spirited and full of cheerfulness as any man could desire. We enjoy it thoroughly. Very many of the young women are exceedingly pretty and dress with rare good taste. We are gradually and laboriously learning the ill manners of staring them unflinchingly in the face—not because such conduct is agreeable to us, but because it is the custom of the country and they say the girls like it. We wish to learn all the curious, outlandish ways of all the different countries, so that we can "show off" and astonish people when we get home. We wish to excite the envy of our untraveled friends with our strange foreign fashions which we can't shake off. All our passengers are paying strict attention to this thing, with the end in view which I have mentioned. The gentle reader will never, never know what a consummate ass he can become until he goes abroad. I speak now, of course, in the supposition that the gentle reader has not been abroad, and therefore is not already a consummate ass. If the case be otherwise, I beg his pardon and extend to him the cordial hand of fellowship and call him brother. I shall always delight to meet an ass after my own heart when I have finished my travels.

On this subject let me remark that there are Americans abroad in Italy who have actually forgotten their mother tongue in three months—forgot it in France. They cannot even write their address in English in a hotel register. I append these evidences, which I copied verbatim from the register of a hotel in a certain Italian city:

John P. Whitcomb, *Etats Unis.*
Wm. L. Ainsworth, *travailleur* (he meant traveler, I suppose) *Etats Unis.*
George P. Morton, *et fils, d'Amerique.*
Lloyd B. Williams, *et trois amis, ville de Boston, Amerique.*
J. Ellsworth Baker, *tout de suite de France, place de naissance Amerique, destination la Grand Bretagne.*

I love this sort of people. A lady passenger of ours tells of a fellow citizen of hers who spent eight weeks in Paris and then returned home and addressed his dearest old bosom friend Herbert as Mr. "Er-bare!" He apologized, though, and said, "'Pon my soul, it is aggravating, but I cahn't help it—I have got so used to speaking nothing but French, my dear Erbare—damme, there it goes again! —got so used to French pronunciation that I cahn't get rid of it—it is positively annoying, I assure you." This entertaining idiot, whose name was Gordon, allowed himself to be hailed three times in the street before he paid any attention, and then begged a thousand pardons and said he had grown so accustomed to hearing himself addressed as "M'sieu Gor-r-*dong*," with a roll to the r, that he had forgotten the legitimate sound of his name! He wore a rose in his buttonhole; he gave the French salutation—two flips of the hand in front of the face; he called Paris *Pairree* in ordinary English conversation; he carried envelopes bearing foreign postmarks protruding from his breast pocket; he cultivated a moustache and imperial, and did what else he could to suggest to the beholder his pet fancy that he resembled Louis Napoleon—and in a spirit of thankfulness which is entirely unaccountable, considering the slim foundation there was for it, he praised his Maker that he was *as* he was, and went on enjoying his little life just the same as if he really *had* been deliberately designed and erected by the great Architect of the Universe.

Think of our Whitcombs, and our Ainsworths and our Williamses writing themselves down in dilapidated French in foreign hotel registers! We laugh at Englishmen, when we are at home, for sticking so sturdily to their national ways and customs, but we look back upon it from abroad very forgivingly. It is not pleasant to see an American thrusting his nationality forward *obtrusively* in a foreign land, but oh, it is pitiable to see him making of himself a thing that is neither male nor female, neither fish, flesh, nor fowl—a poor, miserable, hermaphrodite Frenchman!

Michelangelo*

In this connection I wish to say one word about Michelangelo Buonarroti. I used to worship the mighty genius of Michelangelo—that man who was great in poetry, painting, sculpture, architecture—great in everything he undertook. But I do not want Michelangelo for breakfast—for luncheon—for dinner—for tea—for supper—for between meals. I like a change, occasionally. In Genoa, he designed everything; in Milan he or his pupils designed everything; he designed the Lake of Como; in Padua, Verona, Venice, Bologna, who did we ever hear of from guides, but Michelangelo? In Florence he painted everything, designed everything nearly, and what he did not design he used to sit on a favorite stone and look at, and they showed us the stone. In Pisa he designed everything but the old shot tower, and they would have attributed that to him if it had not been so awfully out of the perpendicular. He designed the piers of Leghorn and the customhouse regulations of Civitavecchia. But here—here it is frightful. He designed St. Peter's; he designed the Pope; he designed the Pantheon, the uniform of the Pope's soldiers, the Tiber, the Vatican, the Coliseum, the Capitol, the Tarpeian Rock, the Barberini Palace, St. John Lateran, the Campagna, the Appian Way, the Seven Hills, the Baths of Caracalla, the Claudian Aqueduct, the Cloaca Maxima—the eternal bore designed the

*Editor title.

Eternal City, and unless all men and books do lie, he painted everything in it! Dan said the other day to the guide, "Enough, enough, enough! Say no more! Lump the whole thing! Say that the Creator made Italy from designs by Michelangelo!"

I never felt so fervently thankful, so soothed, so tranquil, so filled with a blessed peace, as I did yesterday when I learned that Michelangelo was dead.

But we have taken it out on this guide. He has marched us through miles of pictures and sculpture in the vast corridors of the Vatican; and through miles of pictures and sculpture in twenty other palaces; he has shown us the great picture in the Sistine Chapel, and frescoes enough to fresco the heavens—pretty much all done by Michelangelo. So with him we have played that game which has vanquished so many guides for us—imbecility and idiotic questions. These creatures never suspect—they have no idea of a sarcasm.

He shows us a figure and says: "Statoo brunzo." (Bronze statue.)

We look at it indifferently and the doctor asks: "By Michelangelo?"

"No—not know who."

Then he shows us the ancient Roman Forum. The doctor asks: "Michelangelo?"

A stare from the guide. "No—thousan' year before he is born."

Then an Egyptian obelisk. Again: "Michelangelo?"

"Oh, *mon dieu*, genteelmen! Zis is *two* thousan' year before he is born!"

He grows so tired of that unceasing question sometimes that he dreads to show us anything at all. The wretch has tried all the ways he can think of to make us comprehend that Michelangelo is only responsible for the creation of a *part* of the world, but somehow he has not succeeded yet.

Relief for overtasked eyes and brain from study and sight-seeing is necessary, or we shall become idiotic sure enough. Therefore this guide must continue to suffer. If he does not enjoy it, so much the worse for him. We do.

In this place I may as well jot down a chapter concerning those necessary nuisances, European guides. Many a man has wished in his heart he could do without his guide, but, knowing he could not, has wished he could get some amusement out of him as a remuneration for the affliction of his society. We accomplished this latter matter, and if our experience can be made useful to others they are welcome to it.

SOCIABLE ARMENIAN GIRLS

Smyrna has been utterly destroyed six times. If her crown of life had been an insurance policy, she would have had an opportunity to collect on it the first time she fell. But she holds it on sufferance and by a complimentary construction of language which does not refer to her. Six different times, however, I suppose some infatuated prophecy-enthusiast blundered along and said, to the infinite disgust of Smyrna and the Smyrniotes: "In sooth, here is astounding fulfillment of prophecy! Smyrna hath not been faithful unto death, and behold her crown of life is vanished from her head. Verily, these things be astonishing!"

Such things have a bad influence. They provoke worldly men into using light conversation concerning sacred subjects. Thick-headed commentators upon the Bible, and stupid preachers and teachers, work more damage to religion than sensible, cool-brained clergymen can fight away again, toil as they may. It is not good judgment to fit a crown of life upon a city which has been destroyed six times. That other class of wiseacres who twist prophecy in such a manner as to make it promise the destruction and desolation of the same city use judgment just as bad, since the city is in a very flourishing condition now, unhappily for them. These things put arguments into the mouth of infidelity.

A portion of the city is pretty exclusively Turkish; the Jews have a quarter to themselves; the Franks another quarter; so also with the Armenians. The Armenians, of course, are Christians. Their houses are large, clean, airy, handsomely paved with black and white squares of marble, and in the center of many of them is a square court, which has in it a luxuriant flower garden and a sparkling fountain; the doors of all the rooms open on this. A very wide hall leads to the street door, and in this the women sit the most of the day. In the cool of the evening they dress up in their best raiment and show themselves at the door. They are all comely of countenance and exceedingly neat and cleanly; they look as if they were just out of a bandbox. Some of the young ladies—many of them, I may say—are even very beautiful; they average a shade better than American girls—which treasonable words I pray may be forgiven me. They are very sociable, and will smile back when a stranger smiles at them, bow back when he bows, and talk back if he speaks to them. No introduction is required. An hour's chat at the door with a pretty girl one never saw before is easily obtained and is very pleasant. I have tried it. I could not talk anything but English, and the girl knew nothing but Greek or Armenian or some such barbarous tongue, but we got along very well. I find that in cases like these the fact that you cannot comprehend each other isn't much of a drawback. In that Russian town of Yalta I danced an astonishing sort of dance an hour long, and one I had not heard of before, with a very pretty girl, and we talked incessantly, and laughed exhaustingly, and neither one ever knew what the other was driving at. But it was splendid. There were twenty people in the set, and the dance was very lively and complicated. It was complicated enough without me—with me it was more so. I threw in a figure now and then that surprised those Russians. But I have never ceased to think of that girl. I have written to her, but I cannot direct the epistle because her name is one of those nine-jointed Russian affairs, and there are not letters enough in our alphabet to hold out. I am not reckless enough to try to pronounce it when I am awake, but I make a stagger at it in my dreams, and get up with the lockjaw in the morning. I am fading. I do not take my meals now with any sort of regularity. Her dear name haunts me still in my dreams. It is awful on teeth. It never comes out of my mouth but it fetches an old snag along with it. And then the lockjaw closes down and nips off a couple of the last syllables—but they taste good.

Coming through the Dardanelles, we saw camel trains on shore with the glasses, but we were never close to one till we got to Smyrna. These camels are very much larger than the scrawny specimens one sees in the menagerie. They stride along these streets in single file, a dozen in a train, with heavy loads on their backs, and a fancy-looking Negro in Turkish costume or an Arab preceding them on a little donkey, and completely overshadowed and rendered insignificant by the huge beasts. To see a camel train laden with the spices of Arabia and the rare fabrics of Persia come marching through the narrow alleys of the bazaar, among porters with their burdens, money-changers, lamp merchants, Alnaschars in the glassware business, portly cross-legged Turks smoking the famous narghile, and the crowds drifting to and fro in the fanciful costumes of the East, is a genuine revelation of the Orient. The picture lacks nothing. It casts you back at once into your forgotten boyhood, and again you dream over the wonders of *The Arabian Nights;* again your companions are princes, your lord is the Caliph Haroun Al Raschid, and your servants are terrific giants and genii that come with smoke and lightning and thunder, and go as a storm goes when they depart!

The Majestic Sphinx

The sphinx: a hundred and twenty-five feet long, sixty feet high, and a hundred and two feet around the head, if I remember rightly—carved out of one solid block of stone harder than any iron. The block must have been as large as the Fifth Avenue Hotel before the usual waste (by the necessities of sculpture) of a fourth or a half of the original mass was begun. I only set down these figures and these remarks to suggest the prodigious labor the carving of it so elegantly, so symmetrically, so faultlessly, must have cost. This species of stone is so hard that figures cut in it remain sharp and unmarred after exposure to the weather for two or three thousand years. Now, did it take a hundred years of patient toil to carve the sphinx? It seems probable.

Something interfered, and we did not visit the Red Sea and walk upon the sands of Arabia. I shall not describe the great mosque of Mehemet Ali, whose entire inner walls are built of polished and glistening alabaster; I shall not tell how the little birds have built their nests in the globes of the great chandeliers that hang in the mosque, and how they fill the whole place with their music and are not afraid of anybody because their audacity is pardoned, their rights are respected, and nobody is allowed to interfere with them, even though the mosque be thus doomed to go unlighted; I certainly shall not tell the hackneyed story of the massacre of the Mamluks, because I am glad the lawless rascals were massacred, and I do not wish to get up any sympathy in their behalf; I shall not tell how that one solitary Mamluk jumped his horse a hundred feet down from the battlements of the citadel and escaped, because I do not think much of that—I could have done it myself; I shall not tell of Joseph's well, which he dug in the solid rock of the citadel hill and which is still as good as new, nor how the same mules he bought to draw up the water (with an endless chain) are still at it yet and are getting tired of it, too; I shall not tell about Joseph's granaries, which he built to store the grain in that time the Egyptian brokers were "selling short," unwitting that there would be no corn in all the land when it should be time for them to deliver; I shall not tell anything about the strange, strange city of Cairo, because it is only a repetition, a good deal intensified and exaggerated, of the Oriental cities I have already spoken of; I shall not tell of the Great Caravan which leaves for Mecca every year, for I did not see it; nor of the fashion the people have of prostrating themselves and so forming a long human pavement to be ridden over by the chief of the expedition on its return, to the end that their salvation may be thus secured, for I did not see that either; I shall not speak of the railway, for it is like any other railway—I shall only say that the fuel they use for the locomotive is composed of mummies three thousand years old, purchased by the ton or by the graveyard for that purpose, and that sometimes one hears the profane engineer call out pettishly, "D——n these plebeians, they don't burn worth a cent—pass out a king";* I shall not tell of the groups of mud cones stuck like wasps' nests upon a thousand mounds above high-water mark the length and breadth of Egypt—villages of the lower classes; I shall not speak of the boundless sweep of level plain, green

*Stated to me for a fact. I only tell it as I got it. I am willing to believe it. I can believe anything.

with luxuriant grain, that gladdens the eye as far as it can pierce through the soft, rich atmosphere of Egypt; I shall not speak of the vision of the pyramids seen at a distance of five-and-twenty miles, for the picture is too ethereal to be limned by an uninspired pen; I shall not tell of the crowds of dusky women who flocked to the cars when they stopped a moment at a station, to sell us a drink of water or a ruddy, juicy pomegranate; I shall not tell of the motley multitudes and wild costumes that graced a fair we found in full blast at another barbarous station; I shall not tell how we feasted on fresh dates and enjoyed the pleasant landscape all through the flying journey; nor how we thundered into Alexandria, at last, swarmed out of the cars, rowed aboard the ship, left a comrade behind (who was to return to Europe, thence home), raised the anchor, and turned our bows homeward finally and forever from the long voyage; nor how, as the mellow sun went down upon the oldest land on earth, Jack and Moult assembled in solemn state in the smoking room and mourned over the lost comrade the whole night long, and would not be comforted. I shall not speak a word of any of these things or write a line. They shall be as a sealed book. I do not know what a sealed book is, because I never saw one, but a sealed book is the expression to use in this connection, because it is popular.

We were glad to have seen the land which was the mother of civilization—which taught Greece her letters, and through Greece Rome, and through Rome the world; the land which could have humanized and civilized the hapless children of Israel, but allowed them to depart out of her borders little better than savages. We were glad to have seen that land which had an enlightened religion with future eternal rewards and punishment in it, while even Israel's religion contained no promise of a hereafter. We were glad to have seen that land which had glass three thousand years before England had it, and could paint upon it as none of us can paint now; that land which knew, three thousand years ago, well-nigh all of medicine and surgery which science has *discovered* lately; which had all those curious surgical instruments which science has *invented* recently; which had in high excellence a thousand luxuries and necessities of an advanced civilization which we have gradually contrived and accumulated in modern times and claimed as things that were new under the sun; that had paper untold centuries before we dreamt of it— and waterfalls before our women thought of them; that had a perfect system of common schools so long before we boasted of our achievements in that direction that it seems forever and forever ago; that so embalmed the dead that flesh was made almost immortal—which we cannot do; that built temples which mock at destroying time and smile grimly upon our lauded little prodigies of architecture; that old land that knew all which we know now, perchance, and more; that walked in the broad highway of civilization in the gray dawn of creation, ages and ages before we were born; that left the impress of exalted, cultivated Mind upon the eternal front of the sphinx to confound all scoffers who, when all her other proofs had passed away, might seek to persuade the world that imperial Egypt, in the days of her high renown, had groped in darkness.

Arrival of Missionaries

In the breezy morning we went ashore and visited the ruined temple of the last god Lono. The high chief cook of this temple—the priest who presided over it and roasted the human sacrifices—was uncle to Obookia, and at one time that youth was an apprentice-priest under him. Obookia was a young native of fine mind, who, together with three other native boys, was taken to New England by the captain of a whaleship during the reign of Kamehameha I, and they were the means of attracting the attention of the religious world to their country. This resulted in the sending of missionaries there. And this Obookia was the very same sensitive savage who sat down on the church steps and wept because his people did not have the Bible. That incident has been very elaborately painted in many a charming Sunday School book—aye, and told so plaintively and so tenderly that I have cried over it in Sunday School myself, on general principles, although at a time when I did not know much and could not understand why the people of the Sandwich Islands needed to worry so much about it as long as they did not know there was a Bible at all.

Obookia was converted and educated, and was to have returned to his native land with the first missionaries, had he lived. The other native youths made the voyage, and two of them did good service, but the third, William Kanui, fell from grace afterward, for a time, and when the gold excitement broke out in California he journeyed thither and went to mining, although he was fifty years old. He succeeded pretty well, but the failure of Page, Bacon & Co. relieved him of six thousand dollars, and then, to all intents and purposes, he was a bankrupt in his old age and he resumed service in the pulpit again. He died in Honolulu in 1864.

Quite a broad tract of land near the temple, extending from the sea to the mountain top, was sacred to the god Lono in olden times—so sacred that if a common native set his sacrilegious foot upon it it was judicious for him to make his will, because his time had come. He might go around it by water, but he could not cross it. It was well sprinkled with pagan temples and stocked with awkward, homely idols carved out of logs of wood. There was a temple devoted to prayers for rain—and with fine sagacity it was placed at a point so well up on the mountain side that if you prayed there twenty-four times a day for rain you would be likely to get it every time. You would seldom get to your Amen before you would have to hoist your umbrella.

And there was a large temple near at hand which was built in a single night, in the midst of storm and thunder and rain, by the ghastly hands of dead men! Tradition says that by the weird glare of the lightning a noiseless multitude of phantoms were seen at their strange labor far up the mountain side at dead of night—flitting hither and thither and bearing great lava-blocks clasped in their nerveless fingers—appearing and disappearing as the pallid lustre fell upon their forms and faded away again. Even to this day, it is said, the natives hold this dread structure in awe and reverence, and will not pass by it in the night.

At noon I observed a bevy of nude native young ladies bathing in the sea, and went and sat down on their clothes to keep them from being stolen. I begged them to come out, for the sea was rising and I was satisfied that they were running some risk. But they were not afraid, and presently went on with their sport. They were finished swimmers and divers, and enjoyed themselves to the last degree. They swam races, splashed and ducked and tumbled each other about, and filled the air with their laughter. It is said that the first thing an Islander learns is how to swim; learning to walk being a matter of smaller consequence, comes afterward. One hears tales of native men and women swimming ashore from vessels many miles at sea—more miles, indeed, than I dare vouch for or even mention. And they tell of a native diver who went down in thirty or forty-foot waters and brought up an anvil! I think he swallowed the anvil afterward, if my memory serves me. However I will not urge this point.

I have spoken, several times, of the god Lono—I may as well furnish two or three sentences concerning him.

The idol the natives worshiped for him was a slender, unornamented staff twelve feet long. Tradition says he was a favorite god on the Island of Hawaii—a great king who had been deified for meritorious services—just our own fashion of rewarding heroes, with the difference that we would have made him a Postmaster instead of a god, no doubt. In an angry moment he slew his wife, a goddess named Kaikilani Aiii. Remorse of conscience drove him mad, and tradition presents us the singular spectacle of a god traveling "on the shoulder"; for in his gnawing grief he wandered about from place to place boxing and wrestling with all whom he met. Of course this pastime soon lost its novelty, inasmuch as it must necessarily have been the case that when so powerful a deity sent a frail human opponent "to grass" he never came back any more. Therefore, he instituted games called makahiki, and ordered that they should be held in his honor, and then sailed for foreign lands on a three-cornered raft, stating that he would return some day—and that was the last of Lono. He was never seen any more; his raft got swamped, perhaps. But the people always expected his return, and thus they were easily led to accept Captain Cook as the restored god.

Some of the old natives believed Cook was Lono to the day of their death; but many did not, for they could not understand how he could die if he was a god.

Only a mile or so from Kealakekua Bay is a spot of historic interest—the place where the last battle was fought for idolatry. Of course we visited it, and came away as wise as most people do who go and gaze upon such mementoes of the past when in an unreflective mood.

While the first missionaries were on their way around the Horn, the idolatrous customs which had obtained in the island, as far back as tradition reached were suddenly broken up. Old Kamehameha I., was dead, and his son, Liholiho, the new King was a free liver, a roystering, dissolute fellow, and hated the restraints of the ancient *tabu*. His assistant in the Government, Kaahumanu, the Queen dowager, was proud and high-spirited, and hated the *tabu* because it restricted the privileges of her sex and degraded all women very nearly to the level of brutes. So the case stood. Liholiho had half a mind to put his foot down, Kaahumahu had a whole mind to badger him into doing it, and whiskey did the rest. It was probably the rest. It was probably the first time whiskey ever prominently figured as an aid to civilization. Liholiho came up to Kailua as drunk as a piper, and attended a great feast; the determined Queen spurred his drunken courage up to a reckless pitch, and then, while all the multitude stared in blank dismay, he moved deliberately forward and sat down with the women! They saw him eat from the same vessel with them, and were appalled! Terrible moments drifted slowly by, and still the King ate, still he lived, still the lightnings of the insulted gods were withheld! Then conviction came like a revelation—the superstitions of a hundred generations passed from before the people like a cloud, and a shout went up, "the *tabu* is broken! the *tabu* is broken!"

Thus did King Liholiho and his dreadful whiskey preach the first sermon and prepare the way for the new gospel that was speeding southward over the waves of the Atlantic.

The *tabu* broken and destruction failing to follow the awful sacrilege, the people, with that childlike precipitancy which has always characterized them, jumped to the conclusion that their gods were a weak and wretched swindle, just as they formerly jumped to the conclusion that Captain Cook was no god, merely because he groaned, and promptly killed him without stopping to inquire whether a god might not groan as well as a man if it suited his convenience to do it; and satisfied that the idols were powerless to protect themselves they went to work at once and pulled them down—hacked them to pieces—applied the torch—annihilated them!

The pagan priests were furious. And well they might be; they had held the fattest offices in the land, and now they were beggared; they had been great—they had stood above the chiefs—and now they were vagabonds. They raised a revolt; they scared a number of people into joining their standard, and Bekuokalani, an ambitious offshoot of royalty, was easily persuaded to become their leader.

In the first skirmish the idolaters triumphed over the royal army sent against them, and full of confidence they resolved to march upon Kailua. The King sent an envoy to try and conciliate them, and came very near being an envoy short by the operation; the savages not only refused to listen to him, but wanted to kill him. So the King sent his men forth under Major General Kalaimoku and the two hosts met a Kuamoo. The battle was long and fierce—men and women fighting side by side, as was the custom—and when the day was done the rebels were flying in every direction in hopeless panic, and idolatry and the *tabu* were dead in the land!

The royalists marched gayly home to Kailua glorifying the new dispensation. "There is no power in the gods," said they; "they are a vanity and a lie. The army with idols was weak; the army without idols was strong and victorious!"

The nation was without a religion.

The missionary ship arrived in safety shortly afterward, timed by providential exactness to meet the emergency, and the Gospel was planted as in a virgin soil.

Judicious Mr. Rhodes

None of us can have as many virtues as the fountain-pen, or half its cussedness; but we can try.
—*Pudd'nhead Wilson's New Calendar*

The Duke of Fife has borne testimony that Mr. Rhodes deceived him. That is also what Mr. Rhodes did with the Reformers. He got them into trouble, and then stayed out himself. A judicious man. He has always been that. As to this there was a moment of doubt, once. It was when he was out on his last pirating expedition in the Matabele country. The cable shouted out that he had gone unarmed, to visit a party of hostile chiefs. It was true, too; and this dare-devil thing came near fetching another indiscretion out of the poet laureate. It would have been too bad, for when the facts were all in, it turned out that there was a lady along, too, and she also was unarmed.

In the opinion of many people Mr. Rhodes is South Africa; others think he is only a large part of it. These latter consider that South Africa consists of Table Mountain, the diamond mines, the Johannesburg gold fields, and Cecil Rhodes. The gold fields are wonderful in every way. In seven or eight years they built up, in a desert, a city of a hundred thousand inhabitants, counting white and black together; and not the ordinary mining city of wooden shanties, but a city made out of lasting material. Nowhere in the world is there such a concentration of rich mines as at Johannesburg. Mr.

Bonamici, my manager there, gave me a small gold brick with some statistics engraved upon it which record the output of gold from the early days to July, 1895, and exhibit the strides which have been made in the development of the industry; in 1888 the output was $4,162,440; the output of the next five and a half years was (total) $17,585,894; for the single year ending with June, 1895, it was $45,553,700.

The capital which has developed the mines came from England, the mining engineers from America. This is the case with the diamond mines also. South Africa seems to be the heaven of the American scientific mining engineer. He gets the choicest places, and keeps them. His salary is not based upon what he would get in America, but apparently upon what a whole family of him would get there.

The successful mines pay great dividends, yet the rock is not rich, from a Californian point of view. Rock which yields ten or twelve dollars a ton is considered plenty rich enough. It is troubled with base metals to such a degree that twenty years ago it would have been only about half as valuable as it is now; for at that time there was no paying way of getting anything out of such rock but the coarser-grained "free" gold; but the new cyanide process has changed all that, and the gold fields of the world now deliver up fifty million dollars' worth of gold per year which would have gone into the tailing-pile under the former conditions.

The cyanide process was new to me, and full of interest; and among the costly and elaborate mining machinery there were fine things which were new to me, but I was already familiar with the rest of the details of the gold-mining industry. I had been a gold miner myself, in my day, and knew substantially everything that those people knew about it, except how to make money at it. But I learned a good deal about the Boers there, and that was a fresh subject. What I heard there was afterwards repeated to me in other parts of South Africa. Summed up—according to the information thus gained—this is the Boer:

He is deeply religious, profoundly ignorant, dull, obstinate, bigoted, uncleanly in his habits, hospitable, honest in his dealings with the whites, a hard master to his black servant, lazy, a good shot, good horseman, addicted to the chase, a lover of political independence, a good husband and father, not fond of herding together in towns, but liking the seclusion and remoteness and solitude and empty vastness and silence of the veldt; a man of a mighty appetite, and not delicate about what he appeases it with—well-satisfied with pork and Indian corn and biltong, requiring only that the quantity shall not be stinted; willing to ride a long journey to take a hand in a rude all-night dance interspersed with vigorous feeding and boisterous jollity, but ready to ride twice as far for a prayer-meeting; proud of his Dutch and Huguenot origin and its religious and military history; proud of his race's achievements in South Africa, its bold plunges into hostile and uncharted deserts in search of free solitudes unvexed by the pestering and detested English, also its victories over the natives and the British; proudest of all, of the direct and effusive personal interest which the Deity has always taken in its affairs. He cannot read, he cannot write; he has one or two newspapers, but he is, apparently, not aware of it; until latterly he had no schools, and taught his children nothing; news is a term which has no meaning to him, and the thing itself he cares nothing about. He hates to be taxed and resents it. He has stood stock still in South Africa for two centuries and a half, and would like to stand still till the end of time, for he has no sympathy with Uitlander notions of progress. He is hungry to be rich, for he is human; but his preference has been for riches in cattle, not in fine clothes and fine houses and gold and diamonds. The gold and the diamonds have brought the godless stranger within his gates, also contamination and broken repose, and he wishes that they had never been discovered.

I think that the bulk of those details can be found in Olive Schreiner's books, and she would not be accused of sketching the Boer's portrait with an unfair hand.

Now what would you expect from that unpromising material? What ought you to expect from it? Laws inimical to religious liberty? Yes. Laws denying representation and suffrage to the intruder? Yes. Laws unfriendly to educational institutions? Yes. Laws obstructive of gold production? Yes. Discouragement of railway expansion? Yes. Laws heavily taxing the intruder and overlooking the Boer? Yes.